The Seven Principles of Digital Business Strategy

The Seven Principles of Digital Business Strategy

Professor Niall McKeown
Professor Mark Durkin

First published in 2017 by
Business Expert Press, LLC
222 East 46th Street, New York, NY 10017
www.businessexpertpress.com

ISBN-13: 978-1-63157-033-9 (paperback)
ISBN-13: 978-1-63157-034-6 (e-book)

Business Expert Press Digital and Social Media Marketing and Advertising Collection

Collection ISSN: 2333-8822 (print)
Collection ISSN: 2333-8830 (electronic)

Cover and interior design by S4Carlisle Publishing Services Private Ltd., Chennai, India

First edition: 2017

10 9 8 7 6 5 4 3 2 1

Printed in the United States of America.

Dedication

"To Orla, Erinn, Cara and Lily"

—Niall McKeown

"To Deirdre, Matthew and Adam"

—Mark Durkin

Abstract

Strategy creates competitive advantage.
People and a culture of innovation sustain it.
Technology and communications are the means
by which it is delivered.

If we are creating most of our competitive advantage at the strategic planning stage, why are we spending so little time on this and so much time on technology?

This book is not about why you should digitally transform and become more strategic, it's about how. It lays out the steps that must be taken, the data that should be used, and the decision tree to be followed.

Following the principles laid out in this book allows organizational leaders, marketers, and technologists to talk at a high strategic level without getting bogged down in the tactics and delivery that consumes most of the time, attention, and activity in the modern workplace. Use *The Seven Principles of Digital Business Strategy* to define the direction of travel for your business in today's digital economy.

Keywords

business strategy books, business strategy, digital business strategy, digital transformation framework, digital transformation, innovation and entrepreneurship

Contents

Contents

Introduction

In 1971 the NASDAQ was born, and that November, Intel launched the first commercial microprocessor chip, the 4004.

The 4004 is history's first monolithic central processing unit, fully integrated in one small chip. Such a feat of integration was made possible by the use of the then-new silicon gate technology that allowed twice the number of random-logic transistors and an increase in speed by a factor of 5 compared to the incumbent technology.

Since then, chips have improved in line with the prediction of Gordon Moore, Intel's cofounder. According to his rule of thumb, known as Moore's law, processing power doubles roughly every 2 years as smaller transistors are packed ever more tightly onto silicon wafers, boosting performance and reducing costs. Moore's law is thought to be coming to its end due to the physical limits of effects of quantum mechanics, however the rate of change driven by technology is not abating.

A modern Intel processor contains around 3.5 billion transistors, half a million of them would fit on a single transistor from the 4004—and collectively they deliver about 400,000 times as much computing output.

This exponential progress is difficult to relate to the physical world. If cars and skyscrapers had improved at such rates since 1971, the fastest car would now be capable of a tenth of the speed of light causing time distortions for the driver like those seen the movie Interstellar; the tallest building would reach half way to the moon.

While we are nearing the end of super reduction in size of silicon transistors, we are still seeing significant increases in the speed of computing. Today there are 3 billion people carrying smartphones, each one more being powerful than a 1980s' super computer that once filled a space similar in size to a family living room.

The exponential rate of technological advancement means that each morning when we rise, not only are we heading out into a world where more powerful and varied technology exists than existed yesterday—we are moving into a day where more technological advancement will occur than on any other day in history. For business leaders, managing in this ever-changing landscape is challenging enough in itself. Factor in the knowledge that cloud computing and software platforms are increasingly low cost and very powerful, newcomers are emerging all the time, and your competitors have easy access to the same technologies that will engage their customers as well as yours and the challenge is daunting.

Business start-ups require less capital than ever before, and competitors can test new concepts rapidly while maintaining business as usual. The pace of change today is faster than ever before.

Doing business effectively naturally means we must look at the marketplace in which we operate and assess our environment and our competitors. Most businesses do this already, often intuitively, but as the speed of change in the environment increases, being able to turn the resulting data into something more meaningful becomes difficult. In the era of Big Data one enabler for making sense of those data is having the competency to convert the data into information and information into insight. Insight gives us the ability to make management decisions more clearly and quickly based on a timely understanding of market intelligence.

Imagine presenting a spreadsheet full of numbers to an accountant. You ask them for their opinion on the data. They shrug and say it's meaningless. Next you tell them, "It's a profit and loss account and balance sheet." At this point, they can state the obvious characteristics of the report, but the data are still of no great value to either party. Next you ask, "We're considering buying that business, do you think we could reduce its costs and merge it with our business?" The accountant and the data are now able to add value to business decision making. Without the strategic questions and near-term challenges, both the accountant and data are of little use. Put strategy, data, and analysis together and now we have a powerful combination that leads to fact-based decision making.

In a similar context, keeping a close eye on the competition is a critical priority for any leadership team. Knowing what to do with information

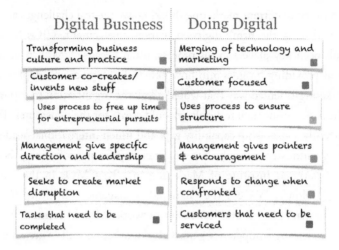

Digital Business	Doing Digital
Transforming business culture and practice	Merging of technology and marketing
Customer co-creates/invents new stuff	Customer focused
Uses process to free up time for entrepreneurial pursuits	Uses process to ensure structure
Management give specific direction and leadership	Management gives pointers & encouragement
Seeks to create market disruption	Responds to change when confronted
Tasks that need to be completed	Customers that need to be serviced

about your competitors is not an automatic consequence of having it, however. Knowing what a competitor is doing, and what technologies they are deploying, is not an advantage in and of itself.

All businesses demonstrate their culture through their behaviors and ways of doing business, but what distinguishes digital businesses is that they are inherently collaborative. For example, digital businesses engage and cocreate with customers to solve challenges and tasks they know exist; they have a sense of ambition and of challenging the status quo—classic qualities of the entrepreneur. They are marketing-oriented and realize that success lies not in what the technology can do but rather in what customers want to do with the technology and that this is where the value exists in that context. Such businesses know that success is all about having a true marketing orientation based on marketing-informed strategy.

While technologists often have a large role to play in ensuring that new digital concepts fly, they are fixers rather than solvers. It is not the responsibility of the technologists to create the vision and strategy of the business. Technologists should be helping to implement a marketing-oriented direction that has been effectively communicated by the leaders. Chief information officers (CIOs), chief marketing officers (CMOs), and chief digital officers have a part to play; ultimately, CEOs and their executive board should guide the decision making and formulate the strategy for change, for opportunity exploitation, or indeed for transformation.

In much of current marketing thinking, we see real challenges around who is driving the firm's digitized market engagement. CIOs have by default been key players in his process, often because CMOs have been poor at providing insights into how new technology can be deployed in a marketing-oriented way that would allow the organization to capitalize on the added value such technology could create for their customer. There is currently a leadership capability gap, and much international academic research, industry research, and commentary from professional bodies [e.g., Chartered Institute of Marketing in UK; CMOs in the United States, Deloitte, WARC, the chartered management institute (CMI), and the management and leadership network (MLN)] continue to evidence increasing competency gaps within marketing staff in areas related to digital technology and its deployment—especially in customer-facing activities and processes.

= DIGITAL TRANSFORMATION

For any digital business, there are prerequisite building blocks that leaders must create if they are to succeed. We argue that the most critical building block, the starting point for any organization wishing to transform themselves into digital innovators, is that of the digital business strategy.

Once the digital business strategy is created, it must be adopted internally and the business aligned to support it. Quite often businesses are not actually blindsided by disruption in the marketplace but rather become aware of it on the horizon, through the media, through business contacts, or through marketing campaigns. It emerges as a graduated process rather than as a more visceral response suggested in the word "disruption" itself. Once managers realize that change is coming to their industry, they understand instinctively that something must be done to counter the disruption and ensure that their own business survives—and thrives—through it. Challenges arise in understanding how best to navigate from the point of identifying a potentially disruptive force to the point of having formulated an effective strategy to counter it. In the context of the pervasive and often disruptive change that digital technology brings to markets, and being mindful too of the digital competency gap identified in marketers internationally, this book provides a framework and sequential process to help navigate the first change block effectively, that of strategy. The framework will provide methods that afford firms the opportunity to understand the shifting landscape as it is moving and see ways of capitalizing on that change more immediately.

On Disruption:

The term "disruptive innovation" when applied to business has become distorted through misunderstanding and misuse. Clayton Christensen was the first person to define organizational disruption in his 1995 book *The Innovators Dilemma*. He explains that not all innovations are disruptive, even if they are revolutionary. For example, the automobile was not a disruptive innovation, because early automobiles were expensive luxury items that did not disrupt the market for horse-drawn vehicles. The market for transportation essentially remained intact until the debut of the lower-priced Ford Model T in 1908.

However, in the past decade, driven principally by Silicon Valley technologists, the term used in common parlance has broadened and is often used to describe a new way of working. It often ignores the Christensen requirements that to be disruptive, the new innovation must be more affordable, effective, and convenient than the predecessor.

For a prime example of what the Valley would call disruption, we need to look no further than the arena of competitive athletics. Anyone with even a passing interest in the high jump event will have heard of a technique called the "Fosbury Flop," where the jumper approaches the bar diagonally, turns, and goes over the bar head first, horizontal to the floor, and backward. The eponymous Dick Fosbury first used this technique in the 1960s, in the face of much skepticism. Prior to this, there was little variation in high jump techniques. Despite their initial skepticism about Fosbury's new technique, his coaches were forced to concede that the technique was superior to anything they'd seen before, when he consistently smashed records during his high school and college years. Fosbury went on to use his technique with great success in athletics competitions, culminating in his taking gold at the 1968 Olympics in Mexico City and breaking the standing Olympic record. At the Olympics in Munich, 4 years later, 28 of 40 high jumpers used the Fosbury Flop technique. Of the Olympians that won medals between 1972 and 2000, almost 95 percent have used the Fosbury Flop technique.

It is accurate to say that Fosbury created disruption within his industry and forever transformed how athletes approach their high jumping technique. This is the same sort of disruption that we perceive in business. Disruption, then, is the discontinuous innovation, rather than a continuous innovation—it represents the creation of a new idea, driving an entirely different way of doing things—a revolutionary change, rather than an evolutionary one, but it would be remiss of us to consider Fosbury's own journey a revolutionary one, without considering the evolutionary method by which he developed and improved the Fosbury Flop technique. Fosbury's personal evolution caused a revolutionary change in the world of athletics.

When we consider this connection between evolutionary change at an individual level and revolutionary change at an industry level, we can translate it to our business leaders. The leaders must evolve himself/herself, and they must be attuned to the emerging trends in their industry or sector and certain at the level of their customers. In short, they must evolve as a marketer to lead success within their company and to preempt the potential disruption that new technology can bring.

Digital disruption is happening all around us, in almost every industry in the world. Because the technologies at our disposal are new, it is tempting to mischaracterize digital disruption as being something for the young, but as we noted earlier, technologies are increasing in number and proficiency at an exponential rate, meaning that in terms of how they relate to business success, the technologies available in industry are often as unfamiliar to the young as they are to the old.

It was a pleasure to visit the headquarters of SAP in Baden-Württemberg, Germany, and meet with the people heading up their innovation department. SAP is one of the biggest enterprise software companies in the world. To give a sense of scale, upon reaching the campus I boarded a bus that drove me through tree-lined streets named after various SAP founders and products. The walks between buildings are long, and the campus accommodates the equivalent population of a small town. While I was talking to the innovation team, they made the astonishing claim that they may no longer be in the software industry in 20 years. I asked them to explain further, and they explained it to me as follows:

Nobody really wants a boiler in their house. Nobody wants plumbing, heaters, or air-conditioning units. Nobody cares for these things. What people want is a constant temperature of 70°F when they're at home and hot water on demand. Ideally, they want these things at a fixed price. The plumbing, boilers, and heaters are a means to reaching this end. Redolent of Levitt's classic essay "Marketing Myopia" and of the need to focus on benefits not on features, SAP is looking to the future as a corporation that intends to create solutions and benefits for their customers, not to develop features for their products. This has a profound effect on how SAP innovates. SAP is attempting to future-proof their business for the next 15 to 20 years by realizing that the innovators of today will be disrupted by the innovators of the future, unless they continually transform.

A short Internet documentary film titled "Humans Need Not Apply," produced by C.G.P. Grey and later featured in The Economist, garnered widespread public attention. Within 2 months of upload, the documentary had received almost 3 million views. In it, Grey examines how technologies, that are already available, or on the horizon, might cause disruption in industry. He demonstrates how no industry is safe—technologies already in existence are coming to displace human workers engaged in everything from coffee making to medical diagnoses.

Grey's film is not the only cautionary tale. Another short film by The Economist, entitled "How Computers Threaten the Jobs of Mid-Skilled Workers," details more ways in which technology might create future disruption in industry. All areas of industry are at risk, it says, and it details ways in which technologies already in development can do manual, cognitive, and even creative work traditionally reserved for human workers.

To deal with this oncoming disruption, businesses will need to transform if they are to stay relevant, survive, and indeed thrive.

Founded in 1996, Google is a company specializing in Internet-related products and services. Gaining initial dominance in the field of search engines, to the point that "Google" is now considered a transitive verb,

Google has branched out and is now part of a larger parent company called Alphabet. It has repeatedly caused—or responded to—industry disruption. In July 2014, the government of the UK announced that from January 2015, it will allow driverless cars to be used on its public roads. Having anticipated and indeed helped shape this eventuality, Google already has a fully developed driverless car (referred to as an "auto") that uses sophisticated lasers, sensors, global positioning system (GPS), and processors to get around safely. In 2014, The California Department of Motor Vehicles insisted that Google installs a steering wheel and pedals into the vehicle before they would pass it as roadworthy—Google didn't see the need. Since then Tesla has advanced faster in this market than the powerful Google.

The next vehicles we buy may not be driverless, but it's looking increasingly likely that the ones we buy after will be—if we even need to own a vehicle at all. The vision is that autos will be automated and ubiquitous. Rather than having a car and the related costs and issues that can come with storing and maintaining it, we may be able to simply hop into and out of autos that transport us around.

This change, from human-operated, gasoline-guzzling vehicles to ones that are powered by electricity and operated by software, will have a profound effect on many industries. How does a car insurance company justify itself, when traffic accidents and car ownership are a thing of the past? How does a gas station profit, when vehicles are largely powered by electricity? How do traffic systems work? What will cities look like when cars can communicate with each other and self-organize, removing the need for traffic signaling? What will happen to public transport? What will happen to retail, mining, logistics, warehousing, and distribution when vehicles are driverless? Who will be the first customers for these new vehicles; how will different sets of consumers and buyers respond to this new innovation; what groups of consumers will be laggards; and to what extent does a residual opportunity remain in serving the needs of these people too? These are not questions for the future; these are questions for now. Within 5 to 10 years, businesses will be forced to respond to these questions with relevant, strategic transformation or potentially face extinction.

To use another example of rapidly approaching disruption, Google and e-commerce giant Amazon are currently developing ways of delivering their products to customers via unmanned aerial vehicles (commonly known as drones). Imagine a world where you're in the middle of cooking dinner and realize that you're out of peas. Rather than having to leave the house and hop into your car (or auto) to go to the store, you can pick up your smartphone and order your peas from a nearby grocery store; 10 minutes later, you are alerted via app that your peas have arrived by drone. You go outside to accept delivery, your peas are winched down to you, and you can continue with cooking dinner. That world is not the future. That world is now—and it has ramifications for businesses. Drone delivery is likely to completely change the way we perceive the procurement of goods, and the businesses that win will be the businesses that effectively transform.

Disruption is not only happening in terms of digital technology and software. Recently, Chinese researchers[1] announced that they have been able to use a method of supercavitation in conjunction with submarines to greatly increase the speed of underwater travel. Put very basically, supercavitation involves the creation of an air pocket around an object in liquid. This air pocket reduces drag on the object (in this case, a submarine) and permits it to travel at much higher speeds. The researchers have tentatively projected that this technology will be available within the next 10 to 15 years.

If supercavitation permits high-speed underwater travel, it has the potential to disrupt the way that we travel and the way that we transport our goods. We've become so accustomed to looking to the skies for faster travel solutions that few people have considered that the next generation of long-distance travel may occur under the seas. The impact on the air travel industry could be huge. Airline companies tend to receive their airplanes up-front and pay for them over following years, so financial difficulty could follow. If underwater travel becomes a popular mode of travel, will we see seaports expanding in the same way that airports have? These are the questions that businesses will need to ask themselves when they're considering future disruptions.

---

[1]See http://www.extremetech.com/extreme/188752-chinas-supersonic-submarine-which-could-go-from-shanghai-to-san-francisco-in-100-minutes-creeps-ever-closer-to-reality.

The medical industry is not immune to disruption either. Ever-increasing computing power is powering the unraveling of the mysteries of genetic code. This is the new field of genomics and it's pointing the way to a new future.

Already it's having an impact on cancer. Mapping the cancer genome is giving hope that a cure to cancer may soon be within reach. New cancer therapies are being created that treat patients based on their cancer's genetic makeup, rather than just on where the tumor is located. Combined with new immunotherapies, these approaches are radically changing how the entire pharmaceutical industry will work in the future. No longer will one pill to cure a problem be considered a reasonable response to a life-threatening disease.

In the near future, a new technique called clustered regularly interspaced short palindromic repeats (CRISPR) will allow scientists to actually edit DNA sequences. It will soon be commonplace that medical practitioners disable key genes in human immunodeficiency virus, deactivate others gone awry in an autoimmune disease like multiple sclerosis, or reprogram yeast DNA to create petrochemicals like plastics.

Genomics is little more than a decade old, but early indications are that dozens of industries and their business models are heading for constant disruption and transformation.

New technologies will transform our industries too. Quantum dots are a new revolutionary material used in electronic devices. They create everything from more efficient computers to cheaper and sharper televisions. Graphene, another nanotechnology material, is increasingly being used to make a wide variety of products from superstrong, but incredibly light, prosthetics to superconducting wires.

Take, for example, the energy industry that makes up 8 percent of gross domestic product. It is predicted that these technologies will reduce the cost of solar power creation to around one-fifth of what it is today. Add to that Tesla's new home battery storage that can harness this natural resource for reuse when needed and we'll see a transformative effect on not just companies but entire markets.

In recent years, we've seen smartphone apps—from the simple to the sophisticated—causing disruption in many industries. Even the most regulated, unionized, legislated professions are vulnerable. One such app is Uber—an app that allows people to use their smartphone to hail a cab to their location. The cab need not be metered, since the Uber app has the ability to measure the distance of the journey via GPS and calculate a price. If there's room in the cab, other passengers can get in or out along the route, reducing the cost to the customer.

This one app was the cause of strikes that took place across much of Europe and the United States, when cab drivers noted a drop in business—a disruption. It would be easy to look at the Uber app and conclude that it is successful because it's a new, smart piece of technology that effectively undercuts a competitor—but that is not quite the whole story. Backers of the Uber app include multinational investment banking firm Goldman Sachs and other organizations, all of whom understand how disruption works. Uber has clearly come from a clinically planned and well-executed strategy, designed to create a point of disruption. Uber was designed to hail cabs and does it very effectively—the strategy was designed to create disruption, and it has.

Here we can see that the technology output (in this case, the app) is only part of the solution—the front-end user interface. This app required a huge amount of strategic planning, investment, and understanding of how the business could grow to take on a market sector that was heavily regulated and very manual. The disruption of these heavily regulated and manual industries drive the point home that no industry is safe.

What are the implications for smaller enterprises with limited resources, shorter planning cycles, and less sophisticated marketing and business skills? How can we take the lessons learned from the big winners and translate them to smaller companies? If you deal with the distribution of goods, from furniture to food and materials, what do you do?

To start with, we must accept that innovation is rarely a single eureka event. It requires compound discovery of new insights, the engineering of solutions around those insights, and then the transformation of an industry or field. Technology does not produce progress by itself; we need to find important problems for it to solve and then must change how we work in order to take advantage of it.

Further on in this book, we will drill down into the details of digital business strategy, but for now, let's look at this simple case study:

Case Study

This is a true story, only the names have been changed in the interest of commercial sensitivities.

Picture a scenario where a local company servicing the hospitality industry suddenly finds itself under threat from a new market entrant that has been growing rapidly in neighboring territory. We'll call this business "New Competitor." We can call the existing local small business "Goods and Stuff."

Goods and Stuff becomes aware that it has a competitor entering its territory. Upon investigating the competitor, the CEO notices that New Competitor has a brand new, state-of-the-art website. Perceiving this as the reason for their rapid growth and potential disruption, the CEO contacts a web designer and commissions a website with roughly the same specification.

New Competitor

When the web designers arrive, they look at the competitor's website for reference:

In response to this threat, the web designers make a very similar website to combat the new force that they perceive will soon engulf their clients as they have done in neighboring territories.

Goods and Stuff's new website uses the identical technology to that of their competitor and takes no chances by mirroring many of the design features of New Competitor.

Within months they realize that their efforts are not halting the advance of New Competitor. Using the Seven Principles of Digital Business Strategy, they soon start to examine their own competitive advantage when compared to that of New Competitor. They don't get beyond the home page of their new market entrant before questions start to emerge.

Your competitor offers next-day delivery—do you?

Your competitor has a 365-day returns policy—do you?

This company stocks around 18,000 products, all available online—do you?

This company will sell to retail and wholesale channels at the same time—can we respond to this apparent conflict in channel distribution?

The answer to all these questions is no. Goods and Stuff has a fleet of vans that travel a delivery route once or twice a week, they offer a 7-day returns policy, they stock around 2,000 products, and most of their sales are made via sales representatives on the road.

Suddenly it's apparent that these two businesses are vastly different. Goods and Stuff is coming from a world of face-to-face selling, with 21 sales representatives on the road, while the competitor is coming from a world of catalog sales. The competitor has momentum that can easily be swung in the direction of online sales and is investing millions because that is its route to market. Goods and Stuff is hoping to invest perhaps $20,000–$30,000 to procure a marketing executive and compete at the same level. The reality is that this strategy is doomed. Goods and Stuff needs to transform.

Goods and Stuff has two options.

Option 1

Look at disassembling its transport logistics systems and switching to something more efficient. Adjust its customer returns policy to something that aligns better with the market. Increase the number of products it stocks, and switch to online-only sales. It must decide if it's going to supply retail and wholesale at the same time and not in some disguised half-hearted two brands (one for retail and one for wholesale) way.

Option 2

Look at a different model entirely, which leverages the advantages of having 21 salespeople on the road compared with the competitor's none. The competitor is having to send out catalogs, while Goods and Stuff can provide solution selling. The competitor has call centers, while Goods and Stuff has face-to-face relationships.

The differences between Goods and Stuff and their competitor may initially be seen as an Achilles' heel, but when we look at the two options, we see that they can be turned into advantages if leveraged correctly. Attempting to compete via Option 1 would be too costly and unlikely to succeed, given the head start of the competitor.

The strategy, then, is for Goods and Stuff to pinpoint and integrate their advantages to overcome the advantages of the competitor, to ensure that the customer values the advantages of Goods and Stuff over the advantages of the competitor.

This sort of strategic analysis leads to business alignment changes, business strategy changes, and cultural changes in an organization. Cultural change is often a stumbling block that requires leadership and management. A change in the culture of a business naturally requires senior leaders to effectively understand, communicate, and lead the change.

One of the challenges we've seen time and time again in businesses small, medium, and large, is that when the emphasis is placed on technology and tactics, this too often displaces the importance of the customer and marketing-led culture change. Two factors appear to compromise the necessary focus on marketing-oriented change; the first is the competency gaps in marketing managers internationally. Being busy "doing marketing" as before, they find it difficult to replace or complement what has been done before with what needs to be done now in the disruptive digital market context. They also lack the necessary digital skills and an understanding of the implications of such digitization on customers and markets. Second, there is a leadership vacuum where issues of generational difference, time pressures, and a fear of "saying the wrong thing" keep senior directors and CEOs nervous about, and distanced from, the digital agenda.

Organizations commonly lack a strategic narrative that is digitally sensitive and in the absence of that narrative executives in the business default to digital tactics—"doing digital."

The following case study illustrates the disconnect.

During a Local Authority Council meeting in the UK, the board discussed—and agreed to—the use of a "pooper scooper" app, which constituents could use to alert the council when a dog walker had failed to clean up after their dog. The app received this board-level attention because the technology was perceived as new and innovative, and the council board members wanted to be perceived as modern and in touch with the digital world inhabited by their constituents. When pressed about what other technology they were employing to keep in touch with their constituents, the board members mentioned Twitter followers,

Facebook friends, and other social media sites, which were overseen by two full-time members of staff.

Upon analysis, it became clear that the pooper scooper app had been downloaded by 0.01 percent of constituents after 18 months. The two full-time staff employed to engage with the constituency through social media were engaging with around 0.3 percent of the constituency.

The board members were putting their emphasis in the wrong place, because the challenges that they faced in engaging with constituents were not properly diagnosed, understood, and translated between the senior management of the council and the information technology and marketing people executing solutions. There was a disconnect between senior management, the needs of the customer, and digital tools. In these situations, the usual response is that budgets are allocated by senior management and given to marketing, technology, and human resources departments, in order to pacify the perception that we need a whole new approach. This typically leads to frantic activity as though the future was unpredictable.

But the future is not entirely unpredictable and even where a degree of unpredictability exists much new thinking in the entrepreneurial marketing space uses effectual logic to propose how differential advantage can be secured in just such unpredictable environments. Management effectiveness in a digitized market environment requires, more than ever before, senior leaders in a business to understand what their vision of the business is, how the customer perceives value residing in that business proposition, and the likely actions of competitors to that proposition.

There are many books written about how to approach digital; "The Lean Startup" by Eric Ries is a fine example for those starting a business. Part of the methodology of the Lean Startup involves the concept of pivoting, which is described by Ries as "structured course correction designed to test a new fundamental hypothesis about the product, strategy, and engine of growth." [p.149] For start-ups, pivoting is a fairly pain-free process, but how would we manage to pivot a business with 500 employees? And why should we pivot?

Very few businesses that start off with a concept and go on to pivot and pivot again win. They are the exception that has been sold as the new rule. In reality, they are not the new rule. The businesses that win are businesses like Uber. The type of business that wins starts off with a very clearly defined value proposition and a knowledge of where they want to take the business. The winners are not going through frenetic, constant change. They have a focus and use data with purpose to help ensure that their strategy is on course. The winners make their strategies with senior management understanding the opportunities, understanding the defined plays, and giving definitive direction to those that matter. Senior managers who succeed at this will manage to stay relevant—those who excel at it will become the creators of industry disruption or will thrive in contexts that are being disrupted by others.

In traditional business frameworks, there is a sequencing and organization of tasks mainly based on predictive logic. In modern-day digital business frameworks, data are more heavily used to understand the marketplace, to understand customer demands, to look at trends and changing trends, to spot disruption in the distance, and to be able to look for new waves and new opportunities for business.

As we discussed earlier, innovation is an essential success ingredient, but the winners and the losers are decided by the success of their innovation-to-execution cycles. As ever, management effectiveness comes from a marriage of thought and action, innovation and execution, and strategy and tactical implementation.

In older businesses that are heavily manual process driven, the real challenge is in making sure that the people within the business understand that the priority is no longer completing the process. The priority now is thinking about how the new digitized economy has impacted on the currency of those traditional processes. The priority now is using insight from customers and trying to imagine in what ways adaptations are needed to maintain market position or to create advantage.

Drawing from over 120 business case studies through Ireland, UK, and Europe as well as academic research over the past two decades conducted in the United States and Australia, this book provides the answer as to how to create digital business strategy. This is essentially business strategy created and implemented through the lens of digital. The environment has become digitized—strategy must follow if organizations are to be successful. By looking through the lens of digital, we propose digital modeling frameworks, we explore and understand business alignment challenges and cultural challenges, and we explore competency gaps that may act as barriers to success in this new context.

We must understand the ground rules and to make a distinction between businesses that do digital and digital businesses. The digital businesses are the ones that are winning. Senior managers can run digital businesses without fully understanding the inner workings of the technology to do so. The Seven Principles of Digital Business Strategy provides a framework where all strategic options are explored and directions proposed and explained. Whatever your business context and whatever your level of digital competency, this book will add value to your business in our digitized economy.

CHAPTER 1

Digital Business Strategy

As was discussed in the Introduction, the world around us is changing at a rapid rate. We can see that more and more technological advancements are encroaching on roles we've historically considered to be ones that could only ever be filled by humans and we understand that the pace of this change is increasing.

Where previously the local superstore employed 30 cashiers to operate 30 cash registers, they now employ a couple of assistants to aid customers with using automated checkout technology. Even in coffee shops, automation is beginning to take over. Despite our ideas about how much we like that friendly barista, preliminary tests by Briggo Coffee—a fully automated coffee bar in Austin, Texas, where you can create your order precisely how you like it and save it for future orders—have shown that people get used to the bot-made coffee quickly and apparently enjoy it no less.

Artificial intelligence is even encroaching on creative jobs such as journalism, law, and accountancy, which were once thought safe from automation.

If companies are to succeed in today's digitized environment, the digital aspects of business can no longer be distinct from the business as a whole, and the strategy of digital business can no longer exist in isolation of broader business strategy. The actions of digital businesses still belong to the tactical marketers and technologists, but the *strategy* of digital business belongs in the boardroom, where the C Suite [i.e., the CEOs, CMOs, CIOs, Chief Finance Officer (CFOs), and Chief Technology Officer (CTOs)] can come together and form a cohesive market-led digital business strategy. This digital business strategy—and the leadership that drives it—is the essential element for success.

The distinguishing characteristics that indicate the onset of disruption are when a current function of a business becomes more affordable, more effective, and more convenient than the current method. Where once a bank would charge its customers for setting up a direct debit, a third party can now handle the transaction by way of a mobile app at a fraction of the cost. While the bank doesn't see this alternative method of payment as a threat in the early days, the fact remains that this is a more affordable, effective and convenient solution for the customer than the bank offers. Because the smaller business markets this feature with greater focus, it has the power to erode the banks dominance in this domain.

Many smaller companies do not necessarily have better technology or processes than larger companies, but the technology and processes they have are more accessible to their customers and customers see more value in the technology-enabled process than in the traditional process. The dilemma, then, lies in how larger businesses can better engage with and understand their customers so that they can deal with these competitors nibbling away at their business. Quite often, these larger businesses are well established—they have a large customer base and large customer value. Clayton M. Christensen argues that making an inferior but more cost-effective product to sell to the customers downstream is the answer—but in today's market this is not the only answer. Christensen argues that technology causes businesses to fall and fail, but as we've discussed, technology is not the full story—technology is only the visible end of the transformation spectrum. By the time technology comes to change how people do things, or causes disruption in an industry, there has already been a huge amount of market sensitivity, culture change, strategy development, innovation, and education within the business using it.

When threatened by these newer, smaller businesses, most businesses respond by pinpointing the technology as the root cause of the disruption they face and then seek to install technology that is similar to, or more advanced than, their competitors, but in order to change businesses in a competitive way, it must be realized that the technologies and processes are only the final piece of a larger puzzle; they are the servants drafted in to answer the questions posed by a broader strategic process. In taking a closer look at this strategy process, we can see that while digital business strategy in and of itself is not the full story, it is the starting block on the track to better, smarter, more competitive business.

Before considering how to utilize technology, we must first understand where it fits within the overall strategic landscape.

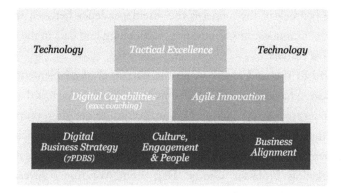

The Change Blocks of Digital Transformation

This model illustrates the high-level change blocks that should be addressed if an organization is to find new and sustaining competitive advantage in the digital world. In this sense, we say that these are the change blocks that must be considered if a business wishes to undergo "Digital Transformation."

In terms of Digital Transformation, we understand the word "Digital" to be a synonym for the pace of change that's occurring in today's world, driven by the rapid adoption of technology. The word "Transformation" describes how an organization is built to change, innovate, and reinvent rather than simply enhance and support the traditional methods.

It shows that digital business strategy cannot be taken in isolation of culture. While this book deals almost exclusively with how to create a digital business strategy, an organization with the best strategy and poor culture is set for failure.

A rough but simple test of organizational culture is to check whether the management blocks access to streaming videos like YouTube or social media sites like Facebook, Twitter, or LinkedIn for their employees. Some managers claim that there are technical or security reasons why this should be so. The reality in most cases however is that the staff are not trusted enough by management to utilize these websites to further their knowledge and build better relationships. An organization with a positive digital culture seeks to provide training to its staff in gaining greater knowledge from YouTube, LinkedIn, and other social platforms rather than discourage their use.

The bedrock of the model is the interdependency between strategy, culture, communications, innovation, technology, and data in the emerging digital context.

Allied to this and representing the next level of enablement is the organization having the necessary competencies and behaviors that allow the business to become agile and innovative. An underlying competency in this dynamic space is the ability to recognize the change process as it is happening and of having the wherewithal to respond in an agile way.

Marketing Professor George Day, from Wharton University in Philadelphia, explained that staff increasingly need what he calls "adaptive" capabilities in facing this digitized economic context. By their nature, these new capabilities are anticipatory and more effectively compensate for the inherent ambiguity and uncertainty in advancing digitized contexts. The open and outward looking nature of these capabilities results in the organization being more innovative and agile in how it anticipates and responds to change and opportunity. Indeed, the increasing attention being paid to design school thinking as applied to business today has much of its roots in the ambiguity and uncertainty managers have been facing in increasingly digitized environments. Thinking more broadly and embracing and leveraging transdisciplinary approaches have been seen to add value to the speed and nature of responses to this level of change. Look at Philadelphia University's new Strategic Design MBA not only as an example of disruption to the traditional and established MBA model but also as an entrepreneurial response to increasing uncertainty in the market and a desire in managers for the development of a different type.[1]

Indeed, a consequence of embracing an approach infused with digital business strategy will naturally expose gaps in education within an organization and identify where capabilities need to be enhanced. One of the key foci in creating a digital business is agile innovation. In her book, *The End of Competitive Advantage*, Rita McGrath, the Columbia business school professor, points out that the challenge of innovation comes from the fact that innovation itself is constant and gaining pace. Businesses that wish to create a strategy that relies on innovation then must change their culture to ensure the constant flow of innovation through the respective

---

[1] See http://www.philau.edu/strategicdesignmba/meet_the_director.html.

organization. She says that one of the most fundamental and recognized notions of business strategy—sustainable competitive advantage—can no longer be a holy grail for companies. Strategy must be combined with the right culture and deliberate cycles of innovation to succeed. While we all understand that the marketing environment is constantly changing (remember PESTEL, the tool for identifying threats and weaknesses used in a SWOT analysis), the speed and magnitude of such change, and the impact on lead times, now make it virtually impossible to respond in a way that allows for sustainable advantage. Deeply ingrained structures and systems designed to extract value, rather than being a competitive advantage, are becoming a liability.

When we look at digital business strategy, and indeed business strategy in general, we must take this into account. We must figure out a way in which to embed natural and constant innovation within our businesses and then go on to ensure that we have the tactical excellence to correctly execute the strategies fuelled by innovation.

Digital business strategy manifests itself by the way of technology-enabled education and data collection married with cycles of focused innovation, which are manifested using technology. Technology is the enabler, not the differentiator. Technology is not the agent of change, but the expression of the leadership thinking and strategy that goes before it. If we successfully execute these ideas with tactical excellence, we can create industry disruption, which leads again to further cycles of transformation through innovation.

Where strategy is market-led, it falls to the business to align the culture, to ensure that the associated capabilities required of the people behind the change imperative are in place, that the business processes are agile and aligned to the strategy and digital environment, and that excellence should emerge in the deployment and implementation of that strategy.

So where do we start in formulating a digital business strategy, and how does it differ from business strategy?

To answer this question, I'll use an example from the courses we run for many of leading thinkers and business leaders. At the beginning of the course on digital business strategy, we hand out paper and ask people to write down their definition of strategy. We then bring these definitions together and look through them. The exercise doesn't last very long, since most people in business have a clear idea of what strategy is. Everyone gets it right in some shape or form. Here are some examples of the answers people have put forward:

1. Strategy is about giving direction.
2. Strategy is about finding the best path to accomplishing a task and achieving a specific goal.
3. Strategy is a plan used to overcome defined challenges where there is a desired outcome.
4. Strategy is about understanding the problem before you start.

None of these definitions can really be faulted. When the definitions are collected, we use them to come up with a single sentence to describe strategy, and it's usually something along these lines:

Strategy is a plan of action to give direction to overcome defined, specific challenges, and in conditions of uncertainty to achieve specific outcomes.

One we have agreed upon a definition; we examine it to see how it fits into different parts of our business.

We'll take junior marketers as an example and examine what sort of strategy they work with, if indeed it can be called strategy at all. Do marketers have a web strategy or a social media strategy? If strategy is a plan of action to achieve goals in conditions of uncertainty, what were the conditions of uncertainty? What were the goals of the web strategy? What were the outcomes? In the courses we run, the tension in the room builds as we consider these questions. When we attempt to look at the work of marketers in this way, what we see is not strategy, but tactics. They are plans similar to those of an architect—complex and intricate—but we don't say that an architect is creating a strategy. We say that she has designed plans.

Vocabulary is important, and often words are used symbolically in business. When we incorrectly identify tactics as strategy, we usually do so to elevate the importance of the tactics we propose. The word strategy gives what we present a gravitas, but of course, this can have a negative impact on the effectiveness of what we want to achieve—or perhaps more accurately—what we think we want to achieve. It makes people in the organization believe that we're being strategic, when we are in fact being tactical. Worse still, these tactics are not coordinated never mind not being set in any overarching framework. It's not strategic marketing, because in these instances, no overriding plan resembling what we call strategy has been given to the wider business. These tactics are important and functional in themselves, but they are not strategic. People like to immerse themselves in tactics because they're more easily and more quickly measured than strategic change and can address the current pressure on immediacy of results and Key Performance Indicators (KPI) achievement. The risk that arises is that such tactics may allow for a degree of efficiency in how we are doing business but undermine our effectiveness in actually what business we are doing. In short, *efficient tactics involves "doing things right"; effective strategy is about "doing the right things".*

Many organizations have a business plan that lays out where they are now, where they need to be, and what way(s) they might get there. In most cases, this business plan is strategic—it explains the direction of travel, predicts and defines the challenges ahead, and calculates the resources that need to be committed. We then surround this business plan with sales strategy, innovation strategy, financial strategy, information technology (IT) strategy, education strategy, recruitment strategy, and marketing strategy.

If we start to examine these strategies, the picture becomes quite complex. To take marketing strategy as an example, when we drill down a little, we realize that things like web strategy, advertising strategy, brand strategy, mobile strategy, social strategy, video strategy, and content strategy are all included under this umbrella, and all these substrategies are only loosely woven together. The IT umbrella includes such things as product development strategy, testing strategy, and implementation strategy. Each of these strategies seem essential for the business—but are they really strategies?

If we look at these "strategies" using the definition of strategy we discussed earlier in this chapter, we can see that they are not strategy—they more closely resemble the architect's plans. These are tactics. All of these tactics and subtactics draw from and give to the business plan—and the business plan, when we look at it in this light, becomes the digital business strategy. Through this lens, we can see that every aspect of the business links into, and is informed by, the digital business strategy. All of our business decisions—every aspect of our tactics—are informed through the lens of digital.

The challenge we most often face when we look at the business plan as digital business strategy is in misunderstanding the word strategy. We often throw out numbers, names, or goals without doing the necessary background work to make sense of them. Here are four examples of things we commonly mistake for strategy.

Expressed Goals

We set goals such as "we will increase our sales by 20 percent. We will increase our page impressions by 10,000 per month."

Having goals as a result of the strategic process is a good thing, but goals in and of themselves are not useful in isolation of that process. In the example above, we need to be asking questions such as the following: What difference will achieving these goals make? Why are they important for the business? Where will the demand come from to meet the goal of 10,000 page impressions per month? Is the market growing, rendering the growth organic, or do we need to do more work to garner these page impressions? How can we increase sales by 20 percent, and what will happen if we don't? Finally, if the targets are not accompanied with guidance on how they can and should be achieved, then this can in no way be considered a strategy.

Operational Effectiveness

In 1996, Michael Porter wrote an article for the Harvard Business Review wherein he claimed that operational effectiveness is not strategy. He talked about the interlinking of technology and systems, which many businesses presumed was their strategic competitive advantage. The same thing is happening today, across the web. Technology systems are being implemented to allow web interfaces to get better access to customer data for marketing automation. This is essentially the digital manifestation of operational effectiveness, often mistaken for strategy.

Interwoven Tactics

Marketers look at their social media and tactical activities and use technology tools to automate the connection between them. They create and embed YouTube videos and other media in their websites and use social media to get the word out about them—and they consider this to be strategic. While they form an essential part of a digital business strategy, these interwoven tactics are not inherently strategic unless they are linked back into the strategic aims of the business, as defined by the digital business strategy.

Power Statements

Everyone who's been in a boardroom has at some point heard these power statements. They usually go along the lines of "we shall use social media to better service our clients."

These statements sound like noble enough goals when uttered in the boardroom, but without strategy to back them up, they are useless, feel-good slogans. Does the statement mean that clients are being poorly served in the first place? Do clients *really* want to talk on social media about private matters? To define channels in this way and construct power statements around them is detrimental. When compared with our definition of strategy, they fall a long way short of the mark.

So far we have defined strategy as *a plan of action designed to achieve a specific goal, in conditions of uncertainty, with defined limited resources.*

Richard Rumelt, the author of the book *Good Strategy, Bad Strategy* in his address to the London School of Economics said, "Good strategy is about defining the nature of the challenge then focus energy and resources on a proximate objective—something that can be accomplished in the near future."

Rumelt suggests, then, that strategy is all about solving near-term critical challenges. He's saying that if we have business assets (i.e., people, plays, and momentum), we should leverage these to create a coherent plan of action and then focus on executing the requisite tactics to solve these issues. Strategy is *not* strategy unless there is coherent action that leads to an outcome that solves the identified problems.

Rumelt goes on to say that strategy has a kernel and that this kernel is made up of three things: diagnosis, guiding policy, and coherent action. For diagnosis, we must ask "why" questions, until we burrow deep enough to understand what challenges the business is trying to overcome. We then select the guiding policy that will help us to understand how we must act to solve those problems or overcome those challenges and the parameters under which we must operate. We then create the guiding policy, which outlines how we will solve the diagnosed challenge—this is usually a set of instructions, which allows the people that will be executing tactical responses to understand clearly what the challenge is, and the parameters in which they should be acting. Finally, we take coherent action to solve the diagnosed challenges. Unless this kernel is present within a set of goals, Rumelt says, the goals cannot be considered strategic.

When a CEO in a business doesn't understand the technological end of digital business because it transforms so quickly, they often task marketers to take care of digital business by making sure that a website is up and running, that social media are being utilized, etc. What we can see then is a set of incoherent actions that are disconnected from any diagnosed challenges or which float in isolation away from the business plan, rather than being informed by it. This usually continues with everyone involved becoming more and more frustrated, because while numbers on a specific graph are going up, the increases are not affecting business change, and competitors always seem to be moving forward.

This misunderstanding of strategy is the first challenge we face. When we bring this into the digital realm and begin to look at business strategy from a digital perspective, we recognize that it is about specifying an organization's goals, opportunities, and related activities. When we lay this over our definition of strategy as put forward by Rumelt, we realize that we are using our vision, goals, opportunities, and related activities to create a set of guiding policies and coherent actions that allow us to solve diagnosed challenges.

A digital business strategy, then, is taking the understanding of strategy and infusing the context in which its development takes place and its actions are implemented with digitization. For the business strategy to work from a digital perspective, we need to understand the management styles that work and the competencies available. We need to get used to the idea of being able to innovate and to test and fail without consequence. This realization leads to a change in business culture, which ultimately needs to be aligned with our strategy if it is to succeed in a digital world.

This change in culture naturally necessitates an adaptation by the people within the business, their roles within the business, and the departments and divisions we've built, sometimes over many years. To align with a digital business strategy, we must be able to effectively manage this culture change. When we change the culture of our business, and consequently the roles of the people within it, we will invariably be left with capability gaps. Education must come to the forefront to help people adjust to new ways of doing business, and those within the business who embrace the change are those who will remain relevant for the organization as we move forward.

Only once we have addressed the management style, culture, alignment and filled in the education gaps are we fit to start considering innovation. If we start to implement innovation too early, before "getting our house in order" as it were, it is likely to be rejected by employees because the business culture is not in the right shape to allow for innovation, and indeed perhaps some of the existing employees are not those who will "fit" with the new digital business strategy.

Innovation has a part to play in digital business strategy, but it cannot jump the queue in terms of sequencing. The alignment of the business, people, culture, and education must come first. When these elements are aligned properly, they lead to inspired, focused innovation that links back to the digital business strategy and drives business growth.

This change of culture and business alignment is no easy task, but it can be done by degrees, piece by piece, as businesses change and have a narrative around change communicated to them (and cocreated with them) by the company. The larger a business is, the more its culture can be ingrained, and the harder the process of change can be. By the same token, for larger businesses with entrenched cultures, in the face of a rapidly changing technological world, the more urgent is the need for change.

In creating a digital business strategy, our ultimate goal is to achieve a plan of action that solves our diagnosed problems, gives us focus, and provides a direction that in turn creates large amounts of momentum. We're creating a strategy that states what the challenges are and what their relative importance is, where we diagnose the critical issues and bring those to our teams, and where we look for our point of leverage and innovate using our existing assets to solve problems. We are aiming for a strategy that gives guiding principles of how to overcome those problems to those who are tasked with tactical response. We want a strategy where the marketing, IT department, and other divisions get on with solving those tactical challenges and deliver value back to the business.

Sandra is the marketing manager of a small software company in Utah. Her marketing strategy contains many promises that in isolation sound like good ideas. Her plan is to use "growth hacking" to gain more "likes" on social media. From there she plans to "push traffic to a landing page." The desired outcome is that anyone who lands on this page will give over their e-mail address, willingly accept the blog articles her team plan to create as a part of their "content strategy," and eventually buy her software. She intends to "build better relationships with potential customers" through constant interaction on Facebook and Twitter.

Shortly after she begins, the realization sets in that her plan is neither strategic nor effective. There is a lot of content already available in her market space. Potential customers don't have an education issue. With nothing unique to say, readers don't feel the urge to give their e-mail addresses and they will in no way be driven like sheep to her landing page, never mind purchasing the software she promotes.

Sandra's business lacks strategic leadership, innovation, and any differentiation that sets her apart from marketplace competitors. Her methods for engaging with customers were based upon leap-of-faith assumptions that potential customers were willing to engage. Her plans didn't start with a clear diagnosis of the situation, and as such her tactical actions were not coherent actions to overcome the diagnosed challenges. Sandra didn't have a strategy. She had a tactical wish list.

Eventually Sandra fixed the problem by getting strategic. She looked at the competitive marketplace, the customer demand, the overall business objectives, and the resources she had at hand. She diagnosed that unless she started with finding a competitive advantage born from innovation that the business couldn't compete.

She worked hard with the software engineers and a pilot customer to create an innovative solution to a common business challenge faced in her customer's industry. This gave her something to go to market with that was different from the competitors and was a starting point for the creation of a real, evidence-based, actionable strategy.

In the digital context, there is a distinct difference between businesses that create digital businesses strategies well and businesses that do not. As outlined in the Introduction, businesses that do it well are digital businesses, and businesses that do not—the more common type of business—are businesses that are simply "doing digital." Sandra's business started off as a business that was doing digital and found her plans, while well meaning, were never going to work.

Businesses that are doing digital believe that the merging of technology and marketing creates advancement and will create success in the new digital world. If they have first mover advantage, or they are leveraging a good brand and have other leveraged assets such as logistics, warehousing, people, and technology, this can work for a short period, but as Rita McGrath pointed out, those things are often short-lived. In a technological world, competitors tend to iterate and catch up quickly, leaving the business outdated. Digital businesses, on the other hand, look to constantly align business culture and practices. They understand that the technology is the delivery agent and that marketing is the way of bringing the solutions enabled by that technology to the people. Moreover, they understand that to get to that point, the business must constantly transform, innovate, and have a culture that is open to transformation ingrained within it.

Businesses that are *doing digital* have websites and social media along with integrated technologies and systems, but the business doesn't really leverage those technologies; instead they often act as a bolt-on to existing functionality. In a *digital business*, the culture dictates that everyone is trying to innovate and transform the business. The people within a digital business understand the culture and the challenges faced by the business, and they seek to change practices to meet those challenges.

Businesses that are *doing digital* talk about how customer-centric they are and how much they care for the customer, but the evidence is lacking. Digital businesses understand that adding value in a digital context is the customer focus required today.

Businesses that are *doing digital* often abide by the "not invented here" philosophy, where they avoid looking outside the business for innovation and ideas. *Digital businesses* drop this pretense entirely and seek out additional value from outside the business, looking to partners, customers, and even competitors for innovation and ideas so that they can understand competitive advantage, create new products or services, and leverage their understanding to create network multiplying effects. Day[2] called this inclusive process "open marketing."

Businesses that are *doing digital* often use processes to ensure that their structures are maintained and working efficiently. This is an essential part of any business, but businesses that are merely doing digital tend to be blinded to changes in using technology, whereas digital businesses constantly look to use processes to add value to the customer experience. If people can be replaced with automation, they are replaced with automation. There is no dispute on this front, because a business that has digital capabilities, that wishes to progress faster and further, has a different approach to technology; it is seen as an opportunity, and not as a threat.

One of the most common failings of businesses that are doing digital comes from senior management. Many believe that they need to

---

[2]G.S. Day. 2011. "Closing the Marketing Capabilities Gap." *Journal of Marketing*, 75, no. 4, pp. 183–195.

understand the minutiae of technology to give proper leadership and direction, so they end up giving pointers and encouragement instead and tasking marketers to meet the challenge. As this book will show, this nuts-and-bolts level understanding of the technologies employed by the business is not necessary. Senior management needs to understand and diagnose the critical challenges facing the business, they need to understand how to overcome these challenges and create a coherent plan of action as to how to overcome those challenges. They need to display leadership in terms of communicating that realistic vision, break it down into key mile markers, and in turn break these into projects and tasks.

In digital businesses, leaders look at their businesses from above and view them holistically, but they also ensure that tactics are being used correctly at ground level to overcome business challenges and ensure that the business is moving forward at a reasonable pace. In digital businesses, leaders realize that their expertise in understanding the broader industry and customer demands, and their ability to use that expertise to strategize as laid out in this book, is what's valuable to the business.

A business that is doing digital responds to change when confronted by industry disruption or even minor change. Change in the industry creates panic in a business that is doing digital, and that panic can lead to poor decisions. Digital businesses anticipate change and thrive on disruption and indeed may seek to create it themselves—they are the change makers and the innovators. Digital businesses have narrowed the capabilities gap, ensured that they have the right culture in place, that they have the right business alignment and that their strategy is entirely geared toward helping them to create disruption.

Businesses that are doing digital tend to lack clear direction from managers. In the absence of direction, they rely on statistical outcomes that may make little sense for the business strategically: likes, page impressions, users, subscribers, and even sales that don't necessarily indicate whether the business is moving in the right direction. Digital businesses can effortlessly marry long-term strategy with the associated short-term tactics needed for implementation. They use data to gain answers. The senior managers of digital businesses do not stay in ivory towers—they get down to the coal face to understand how individual challenges are being tackled within the business and use data to measure how progress matches up to predefined goals and help guide decision making. They use the information they gather along with their expertise to define how the business can progress further.

So, if by these measures we recognize ourselves as wholly or partially a business that is currently *doing digital* rather than existing as a *digital business*, where do we start with digital business strategy?

We must start at the bottom left of the model we looked at the beginning of this chapter—the change blocks of digital business transformation—with the Seven Principles of Digital Business Strategy. While working on our digital business strategy, we must be aware of the fact that it is part of a bigger picture and that it will impact on culture and staff engagement. We must recognize that the business may need to be realigned and that there will be capability gaps. These gaps will need to be filled, these changes implemented, and these challenges met, before we can get into innovation and create tactical excellence using technology.

The chapters of this book take you through the Seven Principles of Digital Business Strategy, showing you where to start, what actions to take, and how to transform the business to meet the demands of an increasingly technological and competitive marketplace. The Seven Principles of Digital Business Strategy is a framework that systematically addresses all three parts of Rumelt's strategy kernel: diagnosis, guiding policy, and coherent action. It takes you through a process of diagnosis, gives guiding policy on the parameters and rules for moving forward, and the likely outcomes associated with those choices, as well as the resources required for any given move allowing the business leaders to make informed decisions and create coherent plans of action that will achieve the desired outcomes leveraging the assets in the business.

CHAPTER 2

An Introduction to the Seven Principles of Digital Business Strategy

In attempting to further our understanding of leadership and management decision making, Walt Disney is very instructive.

His 'Dreamer', 'Realist' and 'Critic' roles are still used in management courses today as illustrations of achieving a balance between what we might achieve if we had no obstacles (the dreamer), the adoption of a more resource-based view (the realist), and a view that challenges decisions made and checks that they are the best they could be in the context of the dream–reality balance (the critic).

In the popular Disney fairy-tale Snow White, we meet the seven dwarfs, a band of well-meaning miniature miners who capture the hearts of not just the heroine herself, but of many generations of readers and viewers. "Can you name all seven dwarfs?" is a question that has appeared on many a trivia quiz for adults—usually with varying results—but we are never asked to name just one of the dwarfs. Indeed, these fairy-tale friendlies are never seen as anything other than a single, heroic body made up of seven very different, but equally valuable and complementary parts. Grumpy, for example, cannot be grumpy without his six companions as his grumpiness is defined by them and their circumstances. For Happy, his happiness infects his colleagues (except Grumpy of course) and the team is better and more effective as a result. Without Happy and Grumpy, they are merely miners going about their business, neither happily nor grumpily, but for both Grumpy and Happy to truly shine as individuals, they must be part of this collective, and for the collective to truly shine, each individual must be present and adding their particular character and personality traits.

So it is with the Seven Principles of Digital Business Strategy although we can't claim these have any particular anthropomorphic qualities. The underlying point is one of *gestalt*—together the Seven Principles are stronger than the sum of their individual parts.

In this chapter, we will give an integrative overview of each of the Seven Principles of Digital Business Strategy. Just as Grumpy is not the completed mining hero without his six counterparts, no one principle of a digital business strategy can stand alone and do the job of the seven. They are all complementary to each other and all necessary if we are to create strategies that can help our businesses to succeed in a modern, technological marketplace. At the end of this chapter, when the seven principles are more clearly defined, we will discuss how they relate to each other.

While the principles are numbered from 1 to 7, it is practical and often necessary for a strategist to start on a principle other than 1 and return to it when they have the right information at hand to complete the task.

The Seven Principles of Digital Business Strategy Are:

1. Know yourself
2. Know your customer
3. Competition
4. Resources
5. Current position
6. Engine of growth
7. Tactics

They can be roughly placed into three different categories, with Principles 1, 2, 3, and 4 making up organizational *internal analysis*, 5 and 6 making up *external analysis*, and 7 being *strategy implementation*.

Internal analysis drills deep into the business and assesses whether we are capable of making the necessary strategic play, macroanalysis is a broader view of where we are in comparison with our competitors and what we can do in order to match or outperform them, and tactics is where we ensure excellence in tactical planning and execution to make sure that our strategy translates into reality and benefits our business.

Internal Analysis

Internal analysis is a review of the inside of your business. This is where you decide what you want out of your business, assess customer demand, look at the competition within the marketplace, and analyze your available resources for forming your strategy. Though each of these four principles is distinct from one another, they are heavily interwoven in the creation of a strategy, and our path to creating a viable, successful strategy can involve revisiting each of these principles as we go along.

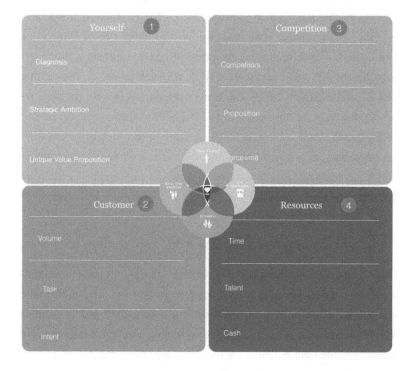

Principle 1—Know Yourself

Within the internally focused stages, the three key elements of the first principle are *ambition*, *diagnosis*, and *unique value proposition*.

It is important to note that the ambition of a business is distinct from its vision, mission, and values. A business vision outlines *where* a company wants to be. It communicates both the purpose and values of the business.

A mission statement talks about *how* you will get to where you want to be. It defines the purpose and primary objectives related to your customer needs and team values. While the vision is essentially "future-oriented" the mission describes the present and how that future position can be reached. This orientation in mission statements makes them useful from a strategy development perspective as they capture and operationalize the sense of ambition (future orientation) that is presented in the vision.

In order to form good strategies, we must have a clear idea of what our business's ambition is—an idea of what we actually want to see happen upon the execution of the digital business strategies we create. As we will see in later chapters, there is a method for creating a business ambition.

Once our ambition is defined, we need to look at our unique value proposition. The unique value proposition of our business is not internally driven—it is not focused on what we want to say, or sell—rather it is focused externally on the customer's perception of what problem we solve, what pain we remove, and what value the customer places on our ability to solve it. We derive our unique value proposition not from what we *believe* our customers should think, nor on how we *believe* our customers should value our products and services—but on how they actually *do* think and on the actual value they place on our products and services.

Principle 2—Know Your Customer

Historically, we have put a lot of effort into considering the demographics of our customers when attempting to classify them. This made sense in the past when more business was done face-to-face and consumers were constrained by geography and technology. In today's digitized world where customers are potentially global in origin, the categories of demography make a more limited contribution.

Indeed, as technology advances, borders are brought down, and as people increasingly use the Internet to conduct business, the time has come to say goodbye to demographics as a way of knowing our customers and to look more closely into the ways customers behave and into understanding what is influencing their behavior. With the spread of Internet technology into every facet of life, people are gaining information and performing tasks in very different ways. Rather than having information thrust upon them and relying on advertising or word-of-mouth to find their nearest provider, customers are coming to the Internet with a specific task in mind, and they are researching products, prices, and providers for themselves. It is this task-based activity that we must explore if we are to know our customers.

Consider, for example, an airline. An airline has no reason to be concerned with the demographics of its customers. Instead, an airline is concerned with any and all customers, regardless of their demographics, whose task is "book a seat on an airplane." Similarly, a company whose sole service is to aid people who wish to start investing is concerned only with the task "begin investing." In both examples, it is the task at hand that is the route to business—not the demographic profile of the customer. What is important is identifying where value can be added in either "taking away the customers' pain" or building in added functionality to task completion that enhances an offering already perceived as valuable.

Evidence of this customer-focused way of doing business exists in the marketplace already, where companies are beginning to unbundle their software and services. Facebook has unbundled its page functionality and its messenger functionality on smartphones, allowing customers to pick one or the other—or both—depending upon the specific tasks they wish to perform. Google has started to unbundle the products in its 'Drive' collection. Rather than downloading a full office productivity suite, a customer can now choose a spreadsheet-only application or a word-processor-only application—again depending on the specific task they wish to perform. This allows us as developers and business providers to become very focused on the customer experience and to capture different users in the moment that they are attempting to perform a specific task.

Principle 3—Competition

In order to understand the competition present in our chosen industry well enough to formulate a cohesive digital business strategy, we must understand digital marketplace dynamics. Imagine Newton's second law of motion, which states that the force of an object depends on both its mass and its acceleration. In the marketplace, this manifests in the way that different businesses of varying sizes, with different momentum, move toward each other. If we are a small business, (the size of a ping-pong ball) and in our marketplace there are larger, more established businesses (the size and weight of bowling balls), there are only very particular circumstances under which we can move the bowling balls enough to get a share of the market.

Although our business is very small in comparison with the bowling ball, if we accelerate quickly enough into the marketplace and with enough force, we may be able to nudge the larger bowling ball just enough to get a small market share. To a small business, this small market share can be a substantial gain. Obviously, our little ping-pong ball is not the only object to which Newton's second law applies. If the bowling ball—the larger business—is also accelerating, it will be far more difficult to move. Similarly, if it is in direct line of the customers we wish to cater to, the nudge we are able to give it may not be enough to gain any market share. In other words, there are circumstances that may make it impossible for us to get a share of the market.

We are able to calculate whether there is a possibility of gaining a share of the market, by understanding the digital marketplace dynamics. We must know who the big players are in the marketplace, what size they are, and what momentum and acceleration they have, if any. We must then look at what force we have available to counter the bigger players and assess whether the market spoils available to us are enough to warrant the fight. Where the firm may find itself limited in its ability to offer a differential advantage, then a decision must be made either to assess the viability of achieving that advantage or, where not viable, in retrenching to a less confrontational market position but where alternative opportunity may be identified.

As the digital footprint of our business and that of our competitors is public information, we have created a formula to calculate both the mass of a brand online and its acceleration in the marketplace. You can compare your force to that of your competitors at this web address:

https://www.ionology.com/dmd

Principle 4—Resources

In management thinking resources were originally classified in economic terms: land, labor, and capital. This relatively narrow definition then broadened to include people, and time (i.e., lead time). More recently still "people" has expanded to include competency and capability in staff.

Interestingly, aspects of "adaptive capabilities" have been heavily focused upon as a key resource in the digitized economy. Adaptive capabilities are essentially those that are anticipatory in nature. These would be commonly found in "externally oriented" organizations, that is, those that adopt an "outside-in" perspective. These organizations are defined by their markets and customers and respond according to changes in these external markets rather than being internally driven and product oriented.

In today's digitized economy, many companies are challenged in having competency sets within the company, including at the level of leaders, which allow for such new opportunities to be defined, exploited, or indeed transformed. A lack of resources however does not mean that opportunities should not be vigorously pursued—entrepreneurial thinking has evidenced that resources will be attracted to viable and exciting opportunities, so there will always be ways of compensating for resource gaps. That said in the digital context we would propose that three main resource considerations exist and these are time, talent, and cash.

When we speak about talent, we are speaking of specialist talents—often leadership talents—meaning that some plays require senior leaders' constant involvement. Talent intensive plans are often associated with the creation of constant cycles of innovation, something that requires constant supervision and leadership, especially in the early years, as the culture of innovation is established.

Once a business becomes efficient at creating, selecting, testing, killing off, or maturing the right innovations that align with the business value proposition, the job of marketing becomes substantially easier. For it is innovation that spreads: tweeters will tweet about the "new innovation," bloggers will blog, and peer review publications will publish if something is innovative. Innovation is most often the catalyst that creates the multiplier effect of great marketing.

External Analysis

This analysis is externally driven—it is about understanding where our business currently sits in the wider context, identifying where we wish to go, finding out what plays are available to us, and defining what we must do to obtain the growth we want.

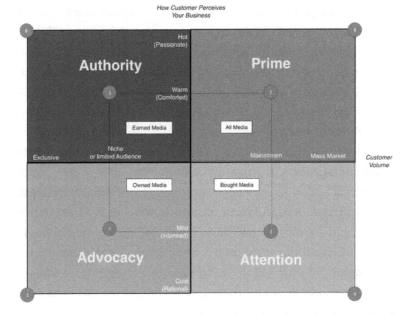

Principle 5—Current Position

Knowing where you are now, where you want to get to, and how to get there is a commonly found underpinning in marketing planning. While easy to conceptualize as correct and sound, in practice this simple model is very difficult to implement, and the apparent simplicity belies a very information-intensive, analytical, and interpretative process around each of the three stages.

Under Principle 5, we will introduce a quadrant that allows us to visualize the different positions in which a business might find itself (where am I now?). The quadrant is split into advocacy, attention, authority, and prime. It is important for us to understand where we are on the quadrant, because our current position will determine what plays might be available to us. Misdiagnosing our position on the quadrant might lead us to prescribe the wrong direction, thereby impacting on our intended destination. In this chapter, we take a detailed look at the characteristics of each position on the quadrant, enabling accurate diagnosis and sound directional policy.

Principle 6—Engine of Growth

The Engine of Growth is, simply put, the defined play or series of plays we need to make to move from our current position on the quadrant (where we are now) to our desired position (where we are going to). There is no "bad" quadrant for any business to be in, but if we wish to move from one position in the quadrant to a different one, we must make the right plays. In the coming chapters, we will take a look at what defined plays are the most likely to move us in the right direction. It is worth noting that each quad has a different corresponding characteristic of growth. An Authority business grows faster than an Advocacy business and Attention business only grow when they can acquire new customers at a price less than the gross margin of the deal. More on this later.

Principle 7—Tactics

Since the tactical response of any given business is almost entirely dependent upon the specifics of its analyses, it is impossible to discuss tactics without the input of some data. In this chapter, we use a case study to

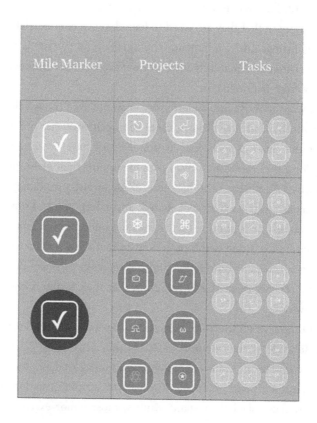

illustrate what a tactical response might look like and to see how our micro- and macroanalyses help us to develop that response.

Tactics typically are responses to unknown values identified within the creation of the digital business strategy. The greater the unknown, the more important it becomes. We start with mile markers—the big issues—and break these down for easy consumption and division into projects and then individual tasks.

Case Study 2.1

At this point in time CKD (Commercial Kitchen Design) is a very strong business sitting in the advocacy quadrant—they've built up their reputation over several years principally by delivering good service and gaining referrals. However, the marketplace is changing, and with other experienced competitors in this quadrant, and increasing commoditization of kitchen equipment and indeed design mean that it is becoming increasingly difficult for CKD to differentiate themselves.

It is common that they are asked to help design a commercial kitchen including fittings and equipment. The challenge they face is that the potential customer demands that they quote the kitchen equipment costs separately from the build cost.

They want to move into an authority position; even though they consider themselves industry experts, there is no evidence that the industry differentiates them as such, and at present they have no unique value proposition. There are also no web data to support their claim that they are perceived as experts. The hallmark of an industry authority is that their ideas area often referenced, shared, and talked about. From a web perspective, no one is quoting them. They have no inbound links.

The current position is also precarious in that the only differentiation is cost, and increased competition and transparency of prices due to the web is reducing margins. CKD recognize that their future is knowledge and innovation.

CKD have a rich source of customer knowledge and understand all the elements of kitchen design. In 2015, they set out their stall at an industry convention, built a demonstration model kitchen, and invited existing customers and potential customers to see their creation. At the tradeshow, they asked their stand visitors, most senior executives, and decision makers, to fill in an anonymous questionnaire. The visitors were asked a wide range of questions regarding what they felt was important when considering the purchase of a commercial kitchen.

The results surprised CKD. Number 1 concern expressed by customers was labor costs of running the kitchen, Number 2 was energy costs, and Number 3 was increasing waste management costs. At the lower end of the survey, the customers showed they had a mild interest in the equipment and kitchen design. They simply assumed the kitchen would be well designed and that the equipment would do the required job.

CKD and the competition had up until now created a proposition based around kitchen design and equipment. This had come about principally because the equipment suppliers force the virtue of their goods through the supply chain that influences the marketing of the service provider.

The evidence from the survey showed there was an opportunity for CKD to change its value proposition, differentiate, and innovate.

Through investment in research they identified energy efficiency, waste management, automation, and personalization of product as key issues, which will need new waves of innovation to allow a commercial kitchen to remain efficient and viable in the future.

While their traditional suppliers were making energy-efficient products, the end purchaser didn't understand what difference the difference between a 300-watt fridge versus a 500-watt fridge really meant in terms of cost reductions. For energy efficiency to make sense a holistic view of energy consumption was required, including expensive energy-guzzling devices such as air extraction fans and gas cooking which was inefficient compared to induction cooking.

These insights led them to consider whole kitchen design and true cost of ownership to be defining issues going forward. These concepts mean that the kitchen of the future will be specifically designed to reduce running costs associated with energy efficiency, waste management, and carbon reduction.

The new kitchen of the future will also be designed to maximize automation through robotics and to allow advances in the personalization of product. CKD understand that they must develop a complete knowledge of the relationships between people, kitchen and restaurant space, air management, equipment, building design, environmental policy, and costs to become industry leaders.

To generate this knowledge, CKD will need planned cycles of focused innovation to develop the concepts of whole kitchen design and the true cost of ownership. They realize that this process will mean rejecting many ideas as well as developing the key ones for innovation. Human stories of new industry-changing innovations make great reading and the industry press is hungry to share content of this nature.

What CKD have discovered is that if they want to break out of the commodity cycle they are in, they must realign their business around new innovations and this in turn creates an opportunity for excellent marketing. If they don't change, marketing becomes increasingly costly and less effective.

They know this will require time, talent, and cash to place them in an authority position with this unique value proposition.

The most important aspect for CKD will be talent, and there will be a need to continue to up-skill the in-house team, but there will also be a need to partner with specific expert disciplines to ensure they become the industry authority. The move from advocacy to authority will require published papers and case studies telling the story of the kitchen of the future. It will require referencing by other industry sources, which will only happen if tried and tested innovations are developed and resourced with the right talent. It is a CKD vision that they find a partner to develop a fully automated and energy-efficient kitchen, which will act as demonstration of the whole kitchen approach.

These concepts have allowed CKD to differentiate themselves through a no extra cost scheme whereby they can gain from increased capital costs of kitchen design by guaranteeing reduced running costs for the client and therefore no extra cost. Their research has indicated that there will be marketing gains from this approach both for them and for the clients.

Through time it is anticipated that other competitors will want to move into this field; however, the position of authority can belong to CKD through an archive of expert knowledge, referenced by the industry and by continuing cycles of innovation.

CHAPTER 3

The First Principle of Digital Business Strategy—Know Yourself

In order to create an effective digital business strategy that will allow us to effect change, and improve our business, we must first understand the business. Knowing yourself is more than having access to data that tell you the current state of things; it is understanding the capabilities of the business in relation to customer desire and marketplace demands and setting realistic goals that will guide us to where we want to be.

We've mentioned before that no single principle of the seven can stand alone. They are all connected and interdependent with one another. Often, addressing one principle can be a catalyst for returning to a principle we have already visited in order to incorporate new information. That said, know yourself can be a good place to start, because we already have all the necessary information immediately available to make our analysis.

Know yourself is made up of two different parts: ambition and value proposition.

Ambition

To understand what we mean by ambition in the context of the Seven Principles of Digital Business Strategy, we must realize that we are discussing the ambition of the strategy itself, rather than the ambition of the business. The word "ambition" is used by management and management consultants often, but usually they are referring to the company's mission (or vision) and values. Mission and values are not irrelevant to digital business strategy—indeed, a business strategy's ambition will often be in pursuit of meeting or furthering a business's mission, or adhering to its values—but the ambition of a strategy is shorter term and informs the strategy's scope.

Relative to a vision, the mission of a business is a short-term desire for its future position. A business's vision is longer term and aspirational, often involving an ultimate destination. The mission of a business explains why it exists. In order to form good strategies, we must have a clear idea of what our strategy's ambition is—an idea of what we actually want to see happen upon the execution of the digital business strategies we create and the mission helps guide that strategic direction more explicitly and immediately.

The values of a business speak to its culture and are displayed daily in the behaviors and interactions of its staff. Businesses usually list their values as being things such as integrity, compassion, innovation, and knowledge—values relate to "how the company does business." Again, an awareness of what sort of culture we wish to create within our businesses is a good thing, and values are an excellent way to convey our cultural desires. In many ways, the values and the manifestation of them in practice help codify the mission of the organization, and in so doing it enables the strategy to be developed, understood, and implemented in line with that mission.

Values require strong leadership if they're to be embedded within a new organization, and that leadership must be present if a business is to keep moving toward achieving its mission. Both are important concepts in successful business, and they both inform the ambition of a strategy, but for a successful strategy we must have a clearly defined strategic ambition.

Ambition is what you plan to achieve in the shorter term, within the strategy, in pursuit of your organization's mission and in keeping with its values. Ambition is important in the digitized economy as it provides an emphasis within strategy development that props up the importance of aiming high and always seeking to aspire to be better. It is an attempt to remove complacency from the equation, always a very present risk particularly in successful enterprises.

Given that the ambition of a strategy must be specific to be effective, we must ask ourselves how we define strategic ambition in larger organizations with multiple departments. We do this by creating a specific digital business strategy for each department. In creating department-specific strategies, we can ensure that the ambition of our strategy is specific and relevant to any given department, such that it can inform effective strategy, while still acting in pursuit of an organization's mission and in keeping with its values. If however a business chooses to digitally transform, it often has to look across business silos. To keep this example simple however, we'll assume that the business is not setting out to transform, simply creating a plan of action that aligns with its existing plans.

To illustrate this, we'll look at the local government of Armagh city in Ireland: Armagh City and District Council (AC DC).

AC DC's mission is to become the most desirable city in Ireland in which to live and the most desirable city in Ireland for tourists to visit. AC DC is up against some very stiff competition, and they're aware of that. As a large organization, they tackle this heavy marketplace competition by ensuring that each division within the organization has a strategy that has an ambition that maintains a focus on propelling the business toward its vision.

Having looked at its resources and at its marketplace, AC DC has pinpointed that, in terms of tourism, it has a vision to become the center for religious tourism in Ireland. It will not reject tourists who visit for nonecclesiastical reasons, but the city holds two cathedrals and is the ecclesiastical capital of Ireland. The Primate of All Ireland (a title denoting ceremonial precedence in the church) resides with the Archdiocese of Armagh, for both the Roman Catholic Church and the Church of

Ireland. AC DC has realized that it is in a prime position to leverage these ecclesiastical attractions in pursuit of its vision. The tourism department's strategic ambition, then, becomes specific to the promotion of ecclesiastical tourism, and in this way, the department remains in pursuit of the organization's higher level vision of becoming the most desirable city for residence and tourism in Ireland.

The dog warden of AC DC has no interest in ecclesiastical concerns as they pertain to the mission of the organization. Instead, the dog warden's strategic ambition, in pursuit of the mission, comes down to ensuring that animals are rescued and rehomed. The leisure department's ambition is to reduce obesity and promote better nutrition and a healthier lifestyle for those who live in the district. This ambition is relevant to those who live in the district, but not necessarily to those who visit. Nonetheless, the department's strategic ambition contributes, in the most meaningful way it can, to the organization's mission. The planning department's ambition is to create the most sustainable environment possible for residents, while maintaining the heritage and architecture that will attract tourists.

All of these ambitions are very different and very specific to each department, its remit, resources, and capabilities, but they are all relevant to the organization's mission, never taking eyes off the higher level goal.

When we understand ambition in this way, we can look at how we form ambitions in relation to the Seven Principles of Digital Business Strategy. A digital business's strategic ambition is often a short-term plan lasting from 3 to 12 months that helps a business move toward its mission and vision. It is used to drive action and to encourage positive decision making. If written effectively, a digital business's strategic ambition will allow participants to do less activity, which is more focused. Their efforts more effectively move toward achieving the strategic ambition, which in turn has a greater impact on working toward the business's vision.

At the core of every effective strategic ambition are three fundamental characteristics—we must be able to communicate them to others, be able to understand them, and be able to measure them. Let's take a look at an example of an effective strategic ambition.

The ambition of the strategy is to help position our company as an industry authority for (insert the company's industry subcategory).

This will be demonstrated when peer-reviewed publications and social media influencers link to us upon launching our (new innovative product or service). This body of work aligns with our ambition because _____.

Setting our ambition out in this way works, because it can be easily communicated to, and understood by, those involved. It has a clear point of measurement (linking and mentions in social media and peer-reviewed publications).

Compare the ambition statement above to this one:

"The ambition of the strategy is to improve our website and leverage social media to create a community. We will use e-mail marketing as well as Pay-Per-Click advertising (PPC) to drive attention and we will measure success by sales conversion."

This ambition statement is less than effective because, rather than being strategic, it is tactical in nature. The strategy is to improve the website (a tactical point) and to leverage social media and create a community (tactical points). There is no context provided as to why or how the community will engage with us. We say that we will use e-mail marketing (a tactic) and PPC (another tactic).

This propensity to outline tactics when tasked with outlining an ambition is very common, but it's a good way to ensure that our strategies become unworkable. As we discussed in Chapter 1, when we looked at Richard Rumelt's *Good Strategy, Bad Strategy*, we are looking to create guiding policy, rather than tactical instruction. The guiding policy should allow those involved in delivering the strategy to understand the parameters.

To use an analogy, when we create guiding policy, we are creating the highway, setting out directions, lanes, and speed guidelines. The guiding policy, or good strategic ambition, doesn't specify the lanes we use, nor the speed at which we drive. In bad ambition, we aim to dictate the style of driving, the exact lanes, used and when. Strategies created in this way can work for a time, but challenges arise when there are obstacles in the road. If we need to switch lanes or change speed to tackle an obstacle, but our guiding policy dictates that we must continue in the same lane and at the same speed with no option to adapt, we are heading for disaster.

Value Proposition

Once our ambition is defined, we need to look at our unique value proposition. This part of the analysis is often misunderstood. The unique value proposition of our business, while it emanates from within the firm (and is therefore internal in origin) is not motivated by internal desires. Rather the value proposition is focused externally on the customer's perception of what we solve and on what value the customer places on our ability to solve it. We derive our unique value proposition not from what we *believe* our customers should think, nor on how we *believe* our customers should value our products and services—but on how they actually *do* think and on the actual value they place on our products and services.

An appropriate value proposition helps us to communicate the value we're delivering to the customer and the customer experience. Put simply, it is a statement of why the customer should buy from us—what service or product they see and the advantage they see in purchasing it from us. It is a business or marketing statement that summarizes why a customer should buy our product or use our service, and the statement should convince a potential customer that our particular product or service will add more value or better solve their problem than any similar offering.

The key to creating an effective value proposition is clarity. We must be clear about what differentiates us from our competition and what makes us the customer's clear choice. While our task during the creation of a digital business strategy is to pin down our unique value proposition, the customer-centric culture and values permeate our business at every level, in every interaction with our customers. The value proposition is the offering through which we convey to our customers the very specific benefits and advantages of doing business with us—and we convey it through multiple modes of communication, from slogans to videos to written communication.

In terms of digital business strategy, the creation of a value proposition is slightly different. Inside the value proposition for a digital business, laser sharp specificity is key.

By having a single point of difference that we specify in our value proposition, we will enable ourselves to potentially build larger market share. It is much easier, in the Internet age, to connect with groups that have shared interests, regardless of how specific they are. Specificity is what will differentiate our businesses from others in the marketplace.

Michael Porter proposes that "Strategy is about making choices, trade-offs; it's about deliberately choosing to be different."

To be unique on the web, where customer choice is almost boundless, we must make tough strategic decisions and pick just *one* thing we wish to emphasize when conveying our value proposition to our customers and communicate this with clarity.

It's important to note that emphasizing one element of our business in our value proposition has no negative effect on other elements of our business. In the case of a city hotel, the value proposition might leverage our cooking, stating our unique feature as "the city's best steak sandwich." We mention our steak sandwich in our communications with our customers, through slogans, headings, and other modes of communication, but none of our potential customers are led to believe that we've done away with beds and stopped serving breakfast. On the contrary, they realize that we still do all of those things and that if they come to stay with us, they will additionally be able to sample the city's best steak sandwich.

People who love a steak sandwich will almost certainly pick our hotel, and people who don't are no less likely to stay with us than they were before. We are now able to focus on those people who have a particular need or desire that plays to the strengths of our business and leverage those strengths as competitive advantages in attracting customers.

The following diagram gives a visual representation of the steps we need to take to create a value proposition for our digital business strategy:

The first step is to create a positioning statement—this is an internal statement where we define what we are best at in *our* world, without looking to the outside world. This internal statement allows us to create effective external marketing messages that accurately convey our strengths to our customers. As mentioned before, for a digital business strategy, this statement of what we're best at must be highly specific and relative. We can then borrow from the book *Zag*, in which Marty Neumeier, referring to this internal positioning statement as an "onlyness" statement, suggests that it can be stated as "our brand is the only _____ that _____."

For the case of our value proposition for digital business strategy, we will use the following structure to account for the necessary specificity:

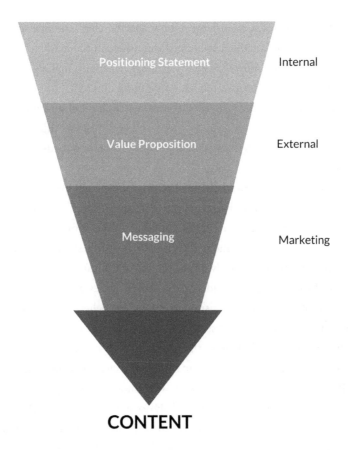

CONTENT

"We are the _____ in _____ for _____ because we do _____ better than anyone else."

So:

"We are the <u>leading provider</u> in <u>a particular field</u> for <u>a specific product/ service</u> because we do <u>our selected element</u> better than anyone else.

Let's have a look at a quick case study of how internal statements such as these can lead to the external statements and marketing messages shown in our funnel diagram.

Case Study 3.1

Damian Maloney is an English entrepreneur who runs a company called Position Field Solutions, which makes software for field service engineers. Throughout the last 15 years, Damian has noticed a change in the way that field service engineers operate. Where they used to be reactive, and respond to what was happening when service calls came in, service engineers started to become more proactive, whereby if a floor's light bulbs were due to fail, they would change the entire floor's bulbs at once to reduce the cost associated with servicing each bulb separately at the point of failure.

In more recent years, Damian has noticed that the area of field service software is becoming very crowded. When he looks at the marketplace, at demand and at competition, he can quickly see, by using analytical keywords tools like Google Adwords, that for field service management software there are a very high volume of searches and that the cost of each Adword click is also very high.

Damian understands that the website to which he is trying to attract customers is very similar to those of his competitors within the marketplace; they talk of reactive and proactive software that permits the management of field services companies.

As a businessman who understands how business works, Damian realizes that all products go through a time during their life cycles where they are considered innovative. A growth period follows, and inevitably the product reaches maturity within the market and eventually goes into decline. The high volume of keyword searches and high cost of Adword clicks in his analytics, when combined, point to market maturity and to current or imminent decline. The market seems to be waning.

Damian can see this is happening in his own marketplace, and he has choices. He can reduce his margins and fight on price, attempting to keep ahead with a decreasing profit margin and an increasing cost per conversion, or he can innovate again.

Having been an innovator for the last 15 years, Damian can spot the next trend coming—a reactive way of working, and reactive software, has led to a proactive way of working, and to proactive software. Having collated data from the industry and done his research, he believes that *predictive* modeling, which will allow field service engineers to be put on site *before* an incident even happens, will be the next wave of innovation.

When creating a strategy for his business going forward, Damian's outlined ambition is to become the UK and Ireland thought leader for predictive field service management.

When he starts to research further, he can see there are peer-reviewed research publications by Oracle and IBM that suggest that his thinking is right. Predictive field management using analytics could be the next big trend in the market for field services management software—but to date, no one has a product in this marketplace. Damian sets to work with his software team trying to understand whether they could lead this wave of innovation in the UK and Ireland if they were to create the software.

Despite the fact this technology doesn't yet exist in the world, Damian keeps his focus on the UK and Ireland market. He understands, when he looks at his resources (which we will discuss as the fourth principle of digital business strategy), that he only has sufficient resource to lead the marketplace in this geographical area. There may be other interested parties that join him in the debate online around predictive analytics and field service management, but his company currently only has the capacity to deliver to the chosen market.

Of course there is inertia within the organizations that provide field services management. Many will make the case that customers are not demanding predictive field services management software, so they have no reason to provide it. Additionally, they will worry over what will happen to the current software they provide that is not predictive.

Damian realizes that he doesn't necessarily wish to speak to all people. Since he will be launching an innovative technology, there will be an early minority who decide to adopt the innovative technology that will in turn make their field services management more innovative. Similarly, there will be a late majority, who will be happy with their current reactive and predictive models. Damian needs to speak to "the innovators"—the 2.5 percent noted in Everett M. Rogers "Diffusion of Innovation" model. The people already looking for a new competitive advantage, who are willing to try new things. He needs to speak to utility providers who want to have greater efficiency in their manpower distribution, who have the wealth to be able to invest in new innovation, and who have the desire to be leading the front end of customer service.

And as to the existing players—Damian's current customers, using the reactive and proactive software what happens to them? The answer is "nothing." They are glad to see that he's innovating and that something new is coming along, and they continue to be customers as before. There is no downside to his innovation in this circumstance.

His internal statement, then, becomes:

We provide the most effective field service management solution because our software is the only tool that predicts future events based on historic data allowing you to deploy resources more cost effectively and improve service.

In this case study, we can see that Damian has created an internal statement. It allows people within the company to focus on defined goals, and it informs the company's ambition. He wants to be first, focus on the UK and Ireland, and provide predictive field services management software. Because they've created the world's first effective predictive modeling solution for field service management in the wider world, in their *internal* world, it means they can start to make some very strong statements about the value of their company (in the context of our funnel diagram, an external value proposition) when it comes to their external marketing messages (the final piece of our funnel).

In external marketing we have to understand the power of context from a digital perspective. People are only on our website reading our messages because they've typed something in to be there. The idea that we have to have full explanations as to everything we do isn't so relevant when we're doing digital business. We have the knowledge that our customers have searched for us, or linked to us, and we have the power of visual cues. Before the Internet, we had to assume that our statements and strap lines *had* to be explicit and explained, visually or otherwise.

The *only* time people will see our headlines and strap lines is in context with other things that are going on in the environment. From a digital perspective, that's typically search referral links, social media, and other commentary that supports our message. Understanding that all our commentary and external marketing pieces are in context with other ongoing actions, Damian can choose a strapline of "predicting tomorrow's field service challenges today" as his primary external message.

Because this context exists in the digital environment, he then has secondary messages he can use, such as a visual representation of the path from reactive to predictive field service management software. Such visual messages can be very simply conveyed. He may then have tertiary messages that explain predictive modeling and software features, but also normal proactive and reactive modeling features. These reactive and proactive products have not gone away, and he's not going to frighten off new people still looking for proactive and reactive software—but he *will* attract a new, additional audience for predictive modeling.

He also finds that when he goes to complete the rest of the strategy in line with the Seven Principles of Digital Business Strategy and aims to become a thought leader, the new and innovative approach is what opens doors. If he wants to speak at a conference, predictive services management software is what people will want to hear about. The innovation will get him a platform, get his content shared, get people talking, and get sales requests coming via the website.

It's that strongly defined ambition and unique value proposition that gives us the ability to propel our businesses forward, and we must have the strength of conviction and leadership to build our strategies around highly specific strengths.

Once we have our ambition and value proposition drafted, and we move on through the rest of the seven principles, we will almost always end up back at the first principle, revisiting and redrafting as we learn more throughout the process. What we must do after every visit is ensure that our ambition and value proposition have COURAGE. They must be as follows:

Concrete—able to define what we do in simple terms.

Obtainable—something we can deliver.

Unique—give us a unique competitive advantage.

Rational—understandable and easily conceptualized.

Actionable—coworkers and customers must be able to take action from it.

Gaugeable—we must be able to measure it.

Explicit—clearly stated, with no room for doubt.

CHAPTER 4

The Second Principle of Digital Business Strategy— Know Your Customer

The second principle is *Know Your Customer*. In a digitized context, this concept relates substantially to customer data dynamics and it can be broken down into three subconcepts: volume, task, and intent.

Before we drill down into the subconcepts of customer data dynamics, it's important for us to realize that knowing your customer is a precursor to the development of a unique value proposition, as outlined in the previous chapter. Should our perspective of volume, task, or intent change, it is highly probable that our value proposition will also require reassessment. This is true in reverse—should our unique value proposition change at any time, we will need to reassess our customer data dynamics to ensure that our strategy has taken everything into account.

Let's take a look at those three subconcepts.

Volume

If we are to create coherent strategy that permits us to achieve tactical excellence, it is vital that we understand customer volume and intent. In Chapter 6, we will discuss the engine of growth within the Ionology quadrant in more detail. The Ionology quadrant allows us to define our approach, identify what plays are available to us, and formulate our strategy for making those plays. Marketplace volume is a key part of understanding what plays are available to us.

Conventional wisdom would tell us that high volume of search in the marketplace for our specific product or service (our task) is a good thing and that low volume is not good—but that's not always the case. Understanding volume is about more than simply discovering what quantity of customers exists. It is about understanding the nature and level of demand which then means looking at the volume and intent of customers in the context of the marketplace and effectively judging our ability to leverage our resources to find a place in the market.

A low customer volume could mean that we have a product or service that nobody wants—but equally, it could mean that the product or service we are looking to provide to customers is innovative and that our customers are not yet aware that it exists. The former may preclude us from entering the market, while recognition of the latter will permit us to formulate our strategy around the recognition that we must raise awareness of the availability of our product or service and convey the relative advantage of that proposition.

By the same token, high customer volumes in our desired marketplace don't necessarily mean that it is a good time to enter that marketplace. A high level of volume is often coupled with a lot of competition. Additionally, a marketplace that has a high level of volume might be approaching maturity, or even entering decline.

When we understand the customer volume that exists in our market-place and why it exists, we can look at it in the context of digital business strategy and understand where we are in the Ionology quadrant. From here, we can better choose what course of action we should take to help us to achieve the ambition we defined under the first principle of digital business strategy.

One of the most readily available tools for measuring volume is Google's Adwords. Google Adwords is not the most accurate desktop tool on the market, but at the time of writing it is the most accessible and cost-effective. The only requirement for using Google Adwords is that the user should have a Google account. The keyword planner tool of Adwords, located under the tools option, has some very interesting and unique features. It allows us to plug in our keywords and then select a specific geographical area, for example. When we come to our macroanalysis and discuss Principles 5 and 6, we will discuss geographical lens locking, and through that, we will understand which geographical areas we may wish to target.

Once we've selected a geographical area, we are able to obtain feedback about how many potential customers are searching in an area and to further narrow those keywords to give us a more accurate picture of what's going on in the marketplace.

To take an example of how high volume in a marketplace can translate into that marketplace being a poor choice for entry, we'll look at orthodontists. In the state of Connecticut there is an average of 880 searches for orthodontists made daily. In New York there are 3,600 searches. This could easily be put down to the difference in population density between Connecticut and New York, but if we look at another area—California—we can see that the number of searches performed daily for the keyword "orthodontist" is disproportionately higher, at 12,100.

What we see here is that there is a five-fold increase from Connecticut to New York, and there is a four-fold increase from New York to California. From a digital perspective, volume is extremely high in California, in comparison with Connecticut, but if an orthodontist is looking to set up a business and compares the volume in the market to the level of competition that exists within that market, we might see that Connecticut could be as good an option as California—if not better—because of the level of competition within the marketplace.

And now for another example, where low volume in a marketplace does not necessarily mean that targeting that market is a bad idea. Form 4 Type 7 switchboards are electrical distribution systems that are used to take high voltages as they come into a data center and break them down into low voltages for use within computer racks. One of the advantages of Form 4 Type 7 switchboards is that each of the cubes that are used to power certain sections of a rack are separated out—this means that if there's a fault in one cube, like a blowout, it has no impact on the other cubes that are within the rack. Form 4 Type 7 switchboards have been used in Europe for some time, but now companies that manufacture them are beginning to target U.S. markets. There is certainly demand as many of larger data centers want to switch to Form 4 Type 7 switchboards, but there are no signs of them going to Google looking for suppliers of it.

In fact, when we look at the Google Adwords results for Form 4 Type 7 switchboards, globally, we can see that there are only on average 10 searches done per day. This doesn't mean that there is no demand, but it does indicate that there would be little point in a business that provides Form 4 Type 7 switchboards attempting to make an attention style play with pay-per-click advertising or Search Engine Optimization (SEO). Rather, for companies selling Form 4 Type 7 switchboards, the apparently low demand portrayed through our Google Adwords data is a sign that business can be done better by using specifically targeted advocacy selling to find our customers.

To summarize, the measurement of volume tells us that if there is low demand, it is an innovation that our potential customers are not yet aware of, that business by advocacy might be a better route to customers, or that the market is in decline and there is little point in attempting to find customers within it. If there is high volume, it tells us that there is an opportunity to make plays later that will allow us to use attention-driven plays and potentially become a prime business, because there is particular demand in our marketplace. In either case, whether the volume we see when using Google Adwords is high or low, we must use the data contextually to decide where we sit in the marketplace.

Task

For many traditional marketers, demographics have long been the holy grail of understanding and targeting customers. Using various indicators, such as age, gender, ethnicity, language, and home ownership status, marketers would attempt to identify specific demographic groups that might purchase the product or service they were offering, to better target them with advertising. With the explosion of the Internet and online business, we see the death of demographics as a tool for identifying potential customers.

For example, cruise vacations have traditionally been marketed toward very specific demographic groups, in particular, the "boomer" woman, the older lady who longs for strolls along the beach in a sarong. Marketers set about selling to this demographic, creating images that portray the boomer lady in a sarong, strolling along a beach, but when we take a look at the demographics, we can see that this picture of the average customer is inaccurate. In fact, there is no such thing as an average customer, in terms of demographic factors. When we try to sell cruises, we find that it is neither the woman nor her desire for long strolls on the beach that actually makes conversions. People choose the cruise and vacations based upon three things—destination, how they can bring parties of people with them, and their ability to relax on the cruise. Their task, then, is the booking of a cruise that goes to a specific location, permits group bookings, and sails aboard a ship that facilitates relaxation. Messaging for this task needs to be specific, and gender is not a viable point of distinction because men book cruises just as often as women. The factors that convert potential customers into customers are those that help them to complete their tasks at hand.

To look at another service, we recently undertook a project where a banking institution wanted to build a new website based on demographics for three stages of life: newly married, saving for college, and retirement. When the data are examined, though, we discover that people are not looking for bank accounts based on their stage of life. Rather, they are looking for bank accounts based on individual needs that are not necessarily affected by, nor reflective of, their demographic characteristics. Customers were looking for convenience tailored to their specific needs. Some wanted the ability to use nearby automatic teller machines, others wanted user-friendly online tools, and yet others were looking for close personal relationships with the bank. The stage of life of the customer was not a factor in deciding which of these was a priority for them.

The best way for this bank to target customers, then, is to target the customers by promoting these specific characteristics and advertising to the people who want them, and not by targeting specific demographic groups and presuming that they desire certain characteristics in their banking experience.

To put it another way, if an architect wanted to sell their services, they wouldn't look for CEOs and they wouldn't attempt to target specific niches or people. They would look at the task the customer comes to them with and seek to respond to that customer task more effectively than anyone else in the marketplace. In the marketplace, we know that people are looking for architects that can make more efficient seating and eating arrangements—say a canteen has a specific seating issue they require a solution for. The architect that is best able to respond to the customer's task of solving the seating issue will get the attention of the customer the quickest. That architect is the one that will receive the contact from the customer. Anyone might be making the call—the CEO of the company, the maintenance manager, or the canteen manager. The business may be large or small. It doesn't matter. The one thing they have in common is that they all have a seating and eating arrangements issue, and the architect best placed to address that issue will get the business.

So we see from these examples that, rather than attempting to sell our products and services to specific demographic groups, in digital business, we must identify what task the customer will be looking to undertake when they do business with us and focus on the ways in which we can be the most effective in the marketplace at allowing them to complete that task.

Intent

Angry Birds Don't Need Therapists

When we seek to understand our customer data dynamics as they relate to digital business, knowing what intention lies behind our customer's decision to perform a specific search is vital if we're to make a good strategy. A recent search for the keyword "angry birds" showed that 36,800 people had searched for the term in 1 month. Without contextualizing these data within the real world, and understanding that Angry Birds is a game, originating as a smartphone app, which has soared in popularity over the last 5 years, we might be led to believe that there is huge demand for veterinary services or bird whisperers to soothe our feathered friends' tempers. Obviously, this would be a huge mistake and exemplifies just how important it is that we make sure that the customer's intent aligns with the capabilities, products, and services of our business.

Let's look at some case studies that demonstrate how a company that has identified high demand and has clearly defined customer tasks might stumble if they misunderstand customer intent.

Case Study 4.1
Certification Europe

Certification Europe is an accredited certification body that provides International Organization for Standardization (ISO) management system certification and other management standards to organizations globally. The business conquered its main territory successfully and wanted to move further through Europe, with specific focus on its certification ISO27001, which is an information security standard. When the business looked at ISO27001, it saw large volumes of customer demand in the marketplace, using keyword data from tools such as Google's Adwords.

To help them to meet the demand for ISO27001 certification in Europe, Certification Europe decided to open a new office to help them better serve their clients. Their intent was to base certification consultants in this office so that they could use attention-driven marketing, such as pay-per-click and SEO, and send consultants out into the field when customers started calling for them.

The first question they had is which country would be the best place to base their office; that is, which geographical area showed the highest demand for ISO27001 certification. Because the search term "ISO27001" is the same in any language, Certification Europe was able to get an immediate picture from the data of where, geographically speaking, the searches were being made from.

Inside Google Adwords, they were able to find the quantity of searches that existed by country. In France, there were on average around 180–220 searches per day. In Germany, there was around twice that volume—360–440 searches per day. This immediately suggested, on the face of it, that Germany would be a better location for Certification Europe to open their new office, assuming the supply level within the marketplace was still low enough to make it viable, but when they looked at the UK, they saw that volume was twice that of Germany—733–896 searches per day.

Within Google Adwords, it is possible to narrow down the geographic area even further. When Certification Europe looked at the data for London, it became apparent that the volume that existed just within a 25 mile circumference around the M25 in London was almost as high as the volume for the whole of France. Logic would tell us that if Certification Europe were to go into a new market, London would be the best place for an office, because it would be the most likely to permit their consultants to effectively serve their customer. So now that they'd used this desktop research to understand demand, and they had defined their task as consultancy and certification for ISO27001, they came to the logical conclusion that their best play would be to open a new office in London, but does this match up to the intent of the customer?

To understand the customer's intent, they must perform a test. The best test that can be used is what we refer to as baseline and base camp testing. With baseline testing, we're trying to find out what the minimum amount of sales opportunities are, if we were to enter the marketplace. With base camp, we aim to ensure that we have a unique value proposition (as defined under the first principle of digital business strategy) by checking it against demand to ensure that our ambition is not misguided. In other words, we are testing our value proposition and ambition against customer intent.

To test for this match, Certification Europe ran pay-per-click ads, because a high level of demand existed within the marketplace and created what's called a minimum viable product. This concept is outlined in *The Lean Startup* by Eric Ries. The concept dictates that we do the minimum amount of work required to answer the leap of faith hypothesis (in this case "we believe that there are people in London who want to get ISO27001 accreditation, and they're looking for consultants online").

We are seeking, with our testing, to prove this hypothesis is true. Certification Europe did this by creating a temporary website and running Google Adwords. The Adwords covered ISO27001 from two different perspectives and allowed the business to see whether their understanding of the customers' motivation matched up to reality.

The first version of the advertisements that were run by Certification Europe advertised help with certification for ISO27001. The second advertised information and training about ISO27001. The click-through rate of those who wanted to get ISO27001 certified (and would therefore be potential customers for Certification Europe) is 3.89 percent. For the advertisements offering training and information, it was approaching 32 percent. This clearly tells us that the vast majority of people searching for ISO27001 are motivated by a need or desire for education and not a desire to actually get certified.

With these data available to us, we work out how many people are searching and how many of those we could potentially attract, work out the cost per search and the likelihood of conversion, and arrive at baseline figures. These figures then easily show us, when we factor in the customer's motivation, that being a digital business in this crowded marketplace is not an economically viable option.

Being a savvy business, Certification Europe recognized that the customer intent did not necessarily match up with their unique value proposition and resourced the project more appropriately. They created websites, supporting sales reps and building brand in the London area. Knowing they had to fight differently to gain a foothold in the marketplace, Certification Europe realized it could not wait on digital to deliver sales opportunities. Rather than ignoring or denying this fact, it acknowledged that this could have a knock-on effect on its growth ambition and started to develop a secondary set of tactics and resources to run alongside digital.

In response to this test, Certification Europe also built a free online education portal to attract new customers seeking knowledge on ISO27001. They understood that if they helped deal with the customers first task, they would be much more likely to be in line to deal with the second, profitable task of helping the organization achieve its ISO objective.

The concept of offering free training was not even a consideration at the outset of creating the digital business strategy. It came about by following the process of the Seven Principles of Digital Business Strategy and seeking to understand customer intent.

Case Study 4.2

Creme Global

For 15 years (at the time of writing), Creme Global has been creating advanced models that allow us to understand the cumulative intake of toxins to the human body. For example, a person brushing their teeth would take in a small, harmless dose of toxin from their toothpaste. If that same person goes on to use lipstick, walks across pesticide-covered grass, and gets into a car, then with each new activity they receive another small dose of various toxins at each point. Creme's models look at the cumulative levels and effects of these toxins over time.

Because Creme's models and modeling software are an innovative technology, little-to-no demand exists for them within the marketplace they see themselves entering. For a decade, Creme has aimed to talk to those who would be potential customers and has found it difficult to reach new clients—usually because their clients do not yet understand the concept or realize that the technology exists. The customer doesn't necessarily know what task they're even attempting to solve—they're not aware that intake modeling across multiple geographies and multiple lifestyles exists. Once the customer does understand, they have a very clear motive, defined roughly as "We want to make our product as safe as possible." The intent of the customer will then revolve around understanding how their products affect the toxin intake of people going about their day.

The first thing the company needs to do is go right back to value proposition and understand that it must now create a new wave in order to create demand within the market. We cannot expect to find motivated clients within the market unless we create demand by raising awareness of our product. To do this, we must be able to clarify which customer task we are able to get done. Taking that into account, Creme starts to take a look at what it could use as a term that will work to effectively create demand. It looks across the web and uses Google search to try and find waves starting to emerge.

One such wave term is around Advanced Consumer Safety Predictive Intake Modeling. This aligned with Creme's desire to create healthier consumer products through their expert, real-world models but we felt the acronym just didn't work. However "predictive intake modeling" as a wave term is something that could create demand and that Creme could "own."

When we start to see scholarly articles being cited for predicting intakes, and using mathematical models, we find that the citations are an indication of a breaking wave, but many in the academic world don't necessarily have the ability to create tasks to align with customer motives, in order to convert them into customers. Creme Global decides that it is going to take up that challenge. It takes the term "predictive intake modeling" and says that this is what they're going to do better than anyone else—they have invented the term and they wish to create demand and make sure the customers have that task at hand.

Competency and Capacity

The challenges both of competency and capacity are evident in these case examples and in understanding how and why staff may or may not get motivated around the digital opportunity. When managers and staff are busy "doing" and not having time to think it is unlikely they will see a need for the new analytical approaches and associated competencies needed in this new context. Many will not have the emerging competency sets needed for managers to envision and exploit what more sophisticated metrics and modeling can bring to their business.

A competency is an underlying characteristic of a person, which results in effective and/or superior performance in a job or the attributes that firms require to be able to compete in the marketplace. A competency is a set of related, but different sets of behaviors organized around an underlying construct, which we call the "intent." Competency also relates to the "personal characteristics" of individuals. This approach focuses on the person and on the characteristics that make people competent.

Managerial competencies have been variously described as the traits, skills, behaviors, and values of effective managers. While managers of a company are significant contributors to its competitive performance, there has been little success in pinpointing the competencies required for a manager to operate successfully in a particular organization.

The context in which the firm operates is also extremely important when considering competency. It is argued that it is unlikely that a single, universal model of competence can be applied to different situations or contexts. Clearly, different industries and types of company have different requirements that influence the particular grouping of skills required of individuals to satisfy those requirements. It has also been proposed that context is important. They have argued that the scope and process of management are not easily isolated from the context in which it takes place. Thus, managerial competencies are closely linked to the context of the organization, its culture, and its environment.

So, in our increasingly digitized marketing environment, it is appropriate to consider if there is a competency base within the firm's marketing team to manage both push and interactive communications through new media such as Facebook and Twitter, and as well as to what extent there is a competency in actually envisioning the potential value of such an engagement. One aspect of this is regulatory compliance, an area that has been considered by many researchers in relation to social media, with suggestions to aid compliance including "clear social media guidelines" and "training staff on social media compliance." In smaller enterprises knowing what to say and when through these new channels can be challenging and time-consuming as can the management of the resulting engagement and ongoing customer dialogue. An organization's culture also influences its competency when undertaking something new. George Day refers to "organizational rigidities" and a "fear of failure" when extending organizations capabilities, while KPMG calls for "something of a culture change" to implement social media effectively. In larger firms, the creation of a digital marketing employee post can prove a disservice to the organization as once again the perception that "digital is different" is perpetuated and inculcated within the culture of the company. In so creating a digital position, digital marketing efforts become separated from "traditional marketing," and this artificial separation can create disconnected customer communications, bring branding challenges, and create issues around managing customer relationships effectively.

In liaising with managers over the past 36 months and in combination with other business development and training activity, we became increasingly convinced that traditional models of marketing training and education were not fit for purpose in an increasingly digitized environment. Traditional teaching and training models in marketing management are characterized by linear and sequential thinking often rooted in a predictive rationale. So, for example, a traditional syllabus may advocate a process of opportunity identification through learning about internal resource potential and environmental audit, market research, new product development (NPD), segmentation, targeting and positioning (STP), planning, launch, and review. Many of these stages are hierarchical in themselves and together they reflect much from "big business" and bureaucratic thinking. As the implementation of such models was discussed in class/seminar contexts with the managers, it became increasingly clear that a gap existed in what such education provided and the usefulness of applying this thinking in the manager's working lives and that over the 3 × 12 month training and education periods this relevance gap was widening. Understanding the aspects of digitized market environments appeared to require a different, nonlinear, and nonsequential thought process and one which was more comfortable in effectual rather than predictive modeling. As these challenges to prevailing teaching approaches in marketing education became more marked over the 36 months, the nature of the required competencies we needed to inculcate in these marketing managers also became an issue for greater exploration. A new competency set has begun to emerge in our thinking and a provisional competency cluster emerged as represented in Figure 4.1.

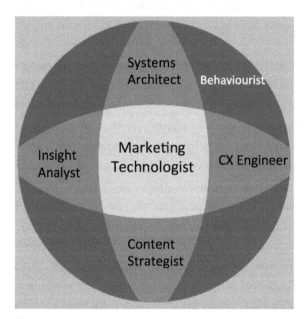

Competency Set

This competency set was inherently interdisciplinary in nature involving thinking traditionally lodged within engineering, art and design, architecture and psychology, as well as in marketing.

Table 4.1 illustrates the characteristics within each role and the emphasis required at a competency level for successful deployment.

Table 4.1 Characteristics of role and issues of competency

Role	What they do	Skills they have	Where to find them
Marketing technologist	Discover, investigate, and prioritize	Curiosity, inner geek, and network	Journalism, large marketing agencies, academia, and information technology functions
Systems Architect	Create single customer view	Systems, data integration, data quality	IT, systems integrators vendors
CX Engineer	Map customer engagement/process blueprinting	Multidisciplinary, customer-attuned, systems design	Consultancy and marketing agencies
Content Strategist	Creation of useful and sustainable messaging materials across platforms	Planning, creativity, and customer empathy	Marketing agency and publishing
Insight Analyst	Predictions, associations, and performance	Curiosity, statistics, and visualization	Data science and marketing
Behaviorist	Discover, experiment, and understand	Economics, psychiatry, and sociology	Consultancy, academic, and megatech

CHAPTER 5

The Third Principle of Digital Business Strategy— Competition

In the book *Who Moved My Cheese? An Amazing Way to Deal with Change in Your Work and in Your* Life by Spencer Johnson, we follow the story of four characters: two mice, Sniff and Scurry, and two tiny people, Hem and Haw, who live in a maze, searching for cheese. The maze is representative of one's environment, while the cheese is representative of one's happiness and success. Through the allegory of the story, where the cheese supply booms and dwindles and moves, we are shown the importance of being ready for change, forecasting change, recognizing when change is occurring and handling change appropriately, and taking preemptive action wherever possible. In the age of digital business, we have more ways than ever before of analyzing the marketplace, and in this chapter we take a look at them.

The ability of a business to cause disruption, particularly a new business entering a marketplace with established players, is often largely dependent on its level of innovation. A new business attempting to enter the marketplace will always be facing challenges.

Because of the way e-commerce works, and the way e-commerce businesses gain customers, it is far more important that we understand this concept in a digital marketplace. It is not impossible for smaller businesses to enter the market by any means, but with larger businesses solidifying their brands by the day, it is imperative that smaller businesses looking to enter the marketplace understand that marketplace well to understand their potential avenue into it.

Competition in the digitized world revolves substantially around digital customer dynamics. To formulate our digital business strategy (now that we have updated our view of customer dynamics from Principle 2), we must update our view of marketplace dynamics. In doing so, we ensure that we utilize the data available to us to make decisions about our marketing proposition and to understand whether we have a competitive advantage or whether it's time to change our strategy to gain advantage.

So what happens to a smaller business in a marketplace of brand giants? How does a new business gather enough acceleration and exert enough force within the marketplace to take a share of it? The answer is to change the industry. Through innovation, the smaller business can avoid going near the larger players at all, by entering and even creating new markets, and ensuring that they are well placed to become the bigger players within them, and we will look at an example of this being done in the following case study.

Case Study 5.1

O'Neills is a very successful sportswear manufacturer in Ireland. They sell as much sportswear as Nike and Adidas and some of the other major players in their marketplace. They are in fact the prime player for sportswear in Ireland and the reason behind this is to do with Gaelic football. Gaelic football is a massively popular amateur sport in Ireland with every town having their own team and their own Gaelic grounds.

This Irish sport requires Irish equipment. Their socks are dyed in Ireland; the footballs are made and hand-stitched in Ireland and every jersey is made in Ireland unlike nearly all other sports where the clothing and equipment are mostly manufactured abroad. Normally this is a low-margin, outsourced, highly commoditized activity.

As the prime player in the market, they are tasked with servicing the demand of their customers. They make all the clothing for the teams and for the supporters. Supporters can go on to their local club website, order the items they want, have them personalized, and then delivered back to the club within a week.

To grow the business, they naturally looked to expand beyond their existing market and into the UK. Although they were the prime player in Ireland, when we change the lens lock to the UK, the picture is very different. They had no brand presence whatsoever and therefore dropped down to the default advocacy position where they had to rely on the slow growth profile of building relationships, knocking on doors, and building up their customer base.

When creating their strategy for growing the business in the UK, they had to form an understanding of the customers and the competitors in this new market which are quite different from Ireland.

Their competitors in the UK were well-established, sizeable brands who had the relationships with the customers, their product offerings were similar to O'Neills' products, and they had plenty of momentum carrying them forward.

When they started knocking on doors and talking to potential customers, O'Neills soon discovered that their unique value proposition was not well matched to their new marketplace, their brand was unfamiliar, and they were easily confused with other O'Neills companies. The UK clubs already had suppliers who would brand their clothing and equipment and deliver the goods back to them. They weren't concerned that the items were made in Ireland. O'Neills soon discover that they don't have a unique offering valued by their customers that differentiates them from their competitors. Trying to break into this new market taking an advocacy route was going to prove incredibly difficult as they didn't have the force to displace their competitors.

An alternative course of action they considered was buying new customers with paid advertising. In this attention section of the quadrant, it's all about product, price, and position. However, they quickly abandoned this particular route as it was going to lead to a bidding war. Because their products don't have a unique differentiator that customers were willing to pay for, they would have to compete on price—a road to nowhere.

The last potential route into this new market they considered was to go for an authority play. Becoming an authority in this marketplace was going to require cultural realignment, time, and innovation. To be an authority in any given market, you need to have other people talking about you and referencing you. The way to do this is through innovation, but innovating in a way that is meaningful to your customers. It means finding some "white space" in which to move thus avoiding trying to displace your larger competitors.

By deciding on the strategy, investing in the right people, introducing processes and cycles of innovation, and getting to know their customers much more closely, O'Neills was able to find a space in the market that gave them the opening they were looking for.

Their innovation was around cut away sections of rugby jerseys that could be infused with menthol. The inspiration came from working closely with schools and helping to solve some of their pains. These cycles of innovation require the strategy and culture to support them and having the right processes in place to score, manage, and implement them.

Through accurate assessment of customer and marketplace dynamics and thorough diagnosis of the challenges they faced, the team at O'Neills was able to formulate a digital business strategy, realign the business, and drive the company to success.

O'Neills took the best of what they had in terms of resources and realigned these toward a new added value opportunity. This approach wasn't traditional in its marketing, but rather effectual in its reasoning.

The synergy that exists between effectual reasoning and digitized marketing provides an opportunity to elevate the marketing concept and shift the mind-set of the marketer.

Effectual reasoning as a new paradigm is still in its infancy, and a better understanding of its constructs is required before it can be measured effectively. The cycle of effectuation starts with the means the entrepreneur has at their disposal (bird in hand principle), comprising who I am, who I know, and what I know. With the means assembled the entrepreneur then determines which effects (goals) are possible (what can I do?)—the second step in the cycle; this is in contrast to causal reasoning that underpins traditional management theory and is characterized by "taking a particular effect as given and focus on selecting between means to create that effect" (Read & Sarasvathy, 2012)[1]. The top-down segmentation–targeting–positioning approach of traditional marketing contrasts with the bottom-up approach of entrepreneurial marketing that starts with a limited base of customers and expands from that point. As part of their "Engagement Project" Google describes how innovative companies (they cite GoPro,

---

[1]Red, S., Sarasvathy, S., Dew, N., Wiltbank, R., and Ohlsson, A-V. (2012), *Effectual Entrepreneurship*, Routledge, Oxon, chapter 5, p.4.

Starbucks, and Amazon) have flipped the traditional marketing sales funnel on its head to create an "engagement pyramid" starting with the 5 percent who are highly engaged and starting from that point. This is not just a question of repeat business from existing customers but also enables new customer acquisition through fostering online influence and advocacy and by tapping into the rich vein of customer knowledge to create new or improved existing products/services, what has been referred to as customer influence value and customer knowledge value, respectively. This contrasts with traditional media, which is designed to generate maximum reach and awareness with the hope that a small percentage of those who respond will drop through the funnel and convert to customers. The engagement-driven strategy is enabled by the high signal strength of new media channels where almost all engagement can be recorded and analyzed, contrasting with traditional media where response is difficult to measure.

In effectuation terms, this technology-enabled knowledge base extends the means the marketer has at his disposal and from which he can imagine goals that are possible.

During the third and fourth steps in the cycle of effectuation, the entrepreneur interacts with people in her network and gains commitments from self-selecting stakeholders who, in a partnership, cocreate and help to shape the new venture. Customers, with whom entrepreneurs interact frequently, are part of that network of stakeholders and can participate in the cocreation of the new venture, product, or service. The video games industry is very innovative in its use of crowdsourcing to develop and enhance games. EA Sports, a division of the global games company, Electronic Arts, partnered with IdeaScale, an open innovation platform, to create a community of nearly 12,000 users, which include their "game changers," which resulted in the generation of more than 7,800 ideas (http://ideascale.com/casestudy/ea-sports). Riot Games uses the social network Reddit, to engage with its users who are able to use the platform to vote on the posts they find most useful. However, crowdsourcing is not just the domain of technology companies; Procter & Gamble claim that crowdsourcing on their Connect & Develop website (www.pgconnectdevelop.com) plays a key role in nearly 50 per cent of its products. In addition to customers, crowdsourcing can extend to suppliers, employees, and citizens—stakeholders in the value constellation. As stakeholders participate, new means are generated which in turn provide the opportunity to realize new goals, thereby continuing the cycle of effectuation.

The growth of social media platforms (e.g., Facebook, Twitter, and Reddit), global review sites (e.g., TripAdvisor and Reevoo), and crowd-sourcing platforms (e.g., IdeaScale and mystarbucks.com) has created an opportunity for organizations to engage with an extended network of engaged users. However, to focus on the technology is to miss the point; what makes this so powerful is the rate of adoption by society and the way in which the technology enables people to do what people like to do—share ideas, tell stories, voice opinions, connect with each other, and consume news.

There are a number of principles, which underpin effectuation including affordable loss. This section explains each principle briefly and discusses the relationship with digitized marketing. The principle of affordable loss debunks the myth that entrepreneurs are inherent risk takers who gamble on the big "all-or-nothing" idea. On the contrary, a founding thinker of effectuation, Saras Sarasvathy, found that entrepreneurs limit risk by understanding what they can afford to lose at each step. This contrasts with causal reasoning, which sets an expected return and then takes steps to minimize risk. The increasing ability, afforded by technology such as software-as-a-service, that allows companies to make modest investments and scale up as demand grows enables this affordable loss principle to be realized. The high signal strength of digital engagement referred to earlier allows organizations to adopt a "test and learn" approach to their marketing, which was not previously possible with the long lead times and up-front investment associated with traditional marketing.

The lemonade principle of effectuation modelling refers to the way in which entrepreneurs embrace change and leverage the opportunities in surprises. This contrasts with the what-if scenario planning associated with causal reasoning, which tries to minimize the probability of unfavorable outcomes. Agile and adaptive companies embrace this principle.

Effectual reasoning and its underlying principles, enabled by technology, provide a framework for marketers in existing (not just start-up) businesses to be entrepreneurial, innovative, and agile.

CHAPTER 6

The Fifth Principle of Digital Business Strategy— Current Position

Where Are We Now?

Foreword

If you have been paying attention up until now, you might very reasonably be expecting this chapter to be about the fourth principle of digital business strategy: resources. Fear not, we haven't lost the ability to count or dropped a Principle. We find that like many of the best combinations in the world, these next three principles make most sense in relation to one another, but in this instance, that comes at the expense of numerical sequencing. Much like sweet only becomes meaningful when compared to salty and sour, and like Grumpy, Happy, and Dopey's distinguishing characteristics really only become apparent in the context of the foibles of the remaining seven dwarves so do Principles 4, 5, and 6 rely on each other for explanation.

Resources are the fourth principle because they form part of the microanalysis, but resources really come into play when it comes to selecting one of the engines of growth. Furthermore, engines of growth only make sense when we understand the quadrant and where we are on that quadrant.

Having said all that, now we can return/skip forward to Principle 5: Where are we now?

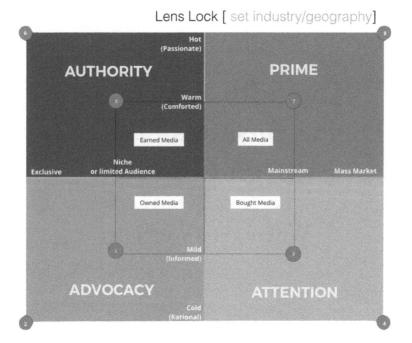

One of the biggest challenges any leader faces is to simply articulate to their teams the current status of their business within a marketplace in comparison with competitors and deciding what to do about it. Being able to bring technologists, marketers, and business leaders together to discuss the current business proposition in a strategic fashion without defaulting to tactical, marketing, or technology discussions is difficult.

This is the Ionology quadrant. It solves that challenge. It is designed to help plot a business' current market position using evidence. We can examine where our business is within a defined marketplace, and as the next chapter will show, we will be able to define where we'd like to take our business in the future and the tactical implications that brings.

Before we can determine how we'd like to grow or transform our business, we must first plot our current standing within our defined marketplace. This chapter deals with how to use evidence to plot a business position within a marketplace.

All strategies need a starting point and a destination. Principle 5 is about defining your starting position. We look at evidence and business characteristics to plot your current position within your chosen market. As you'll see, that will then enable you to clearly articulate a starting position with other team members.

As Alice in Wonderland once discussed with the Cheshire Cat,

Would you tell me, please, which way I ought to go from here?

"That depends a good deal on where you want to get to," Said the cat.

I don't much care where —

Then it doesn't matter which way you go.

Principle 6 is entitled engine of growth; it allows you to plot a new desired destination, a strategic end game. The move we wish to make between our current position and our future desired position determines the actions we must undertake. We cover the available engines of growth in the next chapter.

Naturally with any quadrant there are four key segments: advocacy, attention, authority, and prime. These labels are used to describe how we currently gain new customers. We'll cover this in more detail later.

Each of these positions has very different marketing and growth profile, and the deliberate decision to move from one position in the quadrant to the next will determine the tactical response, resource requirements, communications, innovation requirements, value proposition, and how we obtain new clients. A move in macroanalysis (the quadrant) affects the variables in microanalysis (Principles 1 to 4).

Before we plot our current position on the quadrant we must first add context to the situation. As the quadrant is used to plot not only our current position but also our desired future position, we must constrain our conversations by focusing on a few parameters. We call this setting the "lens lock." A lens lock usually contains two or three of the following variables:

1. A geography— We service the New York state area.
2. A vertical—We operate in the financial services market.
3. A niche within a vertical—We're in the foreign exchange business.

When creating a strategy, the lens lock may change as we hit dead ends or change direction during planning. For instance, James, the CEO of a company named JcoFX, has invented a new predictive modeling software tool he'd like to sell to other foreign exchange traders. He may want to explore what happens if he expands his company into the British market. He may find that there is already a similar product in the UK market that has large momentum and so changes the lens lock to see how a strategy would work if his company became an authority in a new subniche in his hometown.

All strategies are future focused and we set the lens lock to look something like this: New York and London in Financial Services with a special focus on foreign exchange predictive modeling.

The lens lock expresses a desire to expand the business into the London market.

An alternative lens lock could be as follows: New York, financial services, predictive modeling within foreign exchange.

The lens lock can work for simple business propositions also. Maddison sells pies in Alabama via her two retail outlets and she wants consumers around the United States to buy them online.

The lens lock for this business is to grow the territory using digital means. Note she's not trying to sell to the entire world and she is not looking to sell to other retailers. She still wants to target consumers.

For Maddison, this ambitious plan may be a struggle as she'll soon find out when she completes the entire strategy board. The lens lock is very broad for a small business, and while her pies are good, there's no way potential customers in Chicago will be as enthusiastic for her pies without having had the retail experience.

The wider the geography we target, the likelihood of meeting tougher competition increases. The greater the competition, the more resources we usually require to win market share and the more important it becomes to have not just a clear value proposition, but a unique value proposition, something that really differentiates you in your chosen market.

It's easier to differentiate in a smaller market (especially the one you're familiar with) than in a wider market. Innovation powers the creation of unique product and service propositions, enabling businesses to have greater cut-through in a wider market.

The X-axis looks to define the size of the customer base being pursued within a strategy.

Exclusive—indicates that you've got the names and addresses of the people and organizations you want to pursue.

Niche or limited audience—this means we don't know the identities of our target audience, but they can be clearly defined as a subsection of a larger group.

Mainstream—indicates that we want to persuade a large proportion of the defined market of the value of our goods or services.

Mass market—We'd like anyone that's interested in our product or service to know about it.

Here are examples:

Exclusive: We sell outsourced radiology services to 200 potential hospitals in our target geography. We know the names of the hospital CEO and head radiologist.

Niche: We sell health care products to the medical profession, be it hospitals, schools, prisons, and so on in the Boston area. Our target customers are qualified medical practitioners, purchasing managers, and health and safety managers.

Mainstream: We sell health care products to the medical profession, be it hospitals, schools, prisons, and so on all over the United States.

Mass market: We manufacture and sell pain killers to pharmacies and the wholesale channel across the United States.

Notice that the difference between the niche example and mainstream example was simply the size of the market we addressed within our chosen lens lock. In this circumstance, a mainstream market does not always necessarily mean a consumer market. It means that we're choosing to address a broad range of people or a wide geography. Mass market indicates the largest addressable size of a market, while exclusive means a very small addressable size of an overall market.

A familiar tale is for large businesses to choose broad mainstream lens-locked market positions. This can be because growing a $400 million turnover by 5 percent in a year doesn't happen when we focus on small niche markets. However, Wilbur and Orville Wright conquered flight on December 17, 1903. That niche industry grew significantly albeit slowly.

It can take many years for an innovation to become an industry over-night success! The challenge big business has is nurturing innovations that can provide perpetual growth in a period acceptable to their shareholders. Quite often they choose broad "mainstream" markets when they should really focus on building a "niche" market first.

The Y-axis describes how your potential customers perceive your business.

Cold and rational—This indicates that the customer is price-sensitive. Most utility companies have a cold relationship; brand loyalty is often bought with low prices; customers will migrate if a better deal comes along.

Mild and Informed—While the cost of a product or service still matters, there are other conditions a customer considers including a personal relationship, a service differentiator, or location of supply. For example, I may choose a four-star hotel because of its closeness to a conference center. There may be lower cost three-star hotels as well as more expensive five-star hotels but they're too expensive. However, should a better value four-star hotel option appear, I'd take it assuming it's close to the conference center.

Warm and Comforted—The customer and potential customer recognize your brand as a leading authority in your space. Brand warmth is usually created by innovation or repeated consistent advertising. Customers are less price-sensitive and in fact many will pay a premium to be associated with a warm brand.

Hot and Passionate—Customers will pay a high premium for this must-have product or service. An Apple iPhone costs $600 retail, yet it costs around $100 to make. It's in a highly competitive market but still maintains healthy margin and very high demand. It was innovation that drove this appeal. Customers will pay very large premiums for the privilege.

It's possible for a brand to move from cold to hot and back again. Nokia was once a hot brand until it was unseated by the iPhone. It eventually became a mild-informed brand before being acquired by Microsoft.

In 1994 Global Positioning System (GPS) went live. Companies supplying GPS-guided bombs became exclusive/hot suppliers to the military. This technology is now mild/mainstream and no longer demands a premium.

Let's now plot James and his predictive modeling software for foreign exchange and Maddison's pies.

JcoFX predictive modeling software is in use with some customers in New York but has no presence in London. If he settles on a lens lock on the geographic niche of New York and London, it would be fair to say that his product is cold/rational. While innovative, at this moment in time very few customers in this market know anything about the product, particularly in London.

If James was to focus on his home market of New York first and set that as his niche, we could say that the customer would have a mild/informed response to James as they'll be able to reference other users in this limited marketplace.

This nuanced initial position really matters. If James is to make it in both London and New York, his resources (Principle 4) requirement rockets. A move from cold/rational to mild/informed in both the UK and United States may be his desired destination but he may struggle to make either work if the outlook is too broad.

Maddison's pies are considered hot/passionate within a lens lock of a 1-mile radius of her retail shops. When she sets her lens lock to the entire United States, the vast majority of the potential pie market doesn't care who Maddison is. They'll struggle to find her and she'll struggle to build a brand online without customers having the retail experience first. Her newly defined position in her chosen lens lock is cold/rational and mainstream. This is not where she wants to be, it's too price-sensitive. She wants to be warm/comforted and mainstream. Unfortunately, it's not her choice but that of the customer.

To service this lens lock may require serious investment if Maddison is to sell her luxury pies at a premium price on the web. Alternatively, she may wish to consider a smaller identified market and grow her business by combining her retail expertise and opening more shops, combined with online ordering.

Advocacy/Authority/Attention and Prime

There are eight points marked on the Ionology quadrant. Each quad contains two possible plot points that could match your business profile. Before we find our exact plot point we must first find which of the four main quadrants best match our current business characteristics.

Advocacy, authority, attention, and prime describe how businesses gain new customers.

Advocacy

The default position for most businesses:

Sales tend to happen because a sales representative proactively seeks customers for their product. Personal relationship building over a long period is an essential driver of business growth and many sales opportunities come from recommendations of happy customers. They market to existing customers using e-mail marketing and social media channels mostly.

Attention

Paying for attention:

While maintaining many of the same features of advocacy, some businesses advertise a product or service. Attention techniques include search engine advertising and optimization as well as attending trade shows, sponsorship, and display advertising. They spend cash on customer acquisition.

Authority

Earned media, inbound links, and social media shares due to repeated innovation:

Many niche businesses invent new industry categories or subcategories. They invent a thing worth sharing which creates a story worth telling and they contribute something that others want to talk about. They lead a group of like-minded individuals passionate about their subcategory by creating insights and value.

If the invention is indeed newsworthy, it will spread without advertising. The business can become an industry authority. It is authority leaders that create and lead the best communities, get shared the most on social media, get referenced in academic journals, and get paid to speak at international conferences. Customers come to them because of who they are, what they stand for, and they seek to align with the authority innovation and use it to their own advantage.

Prime

Mature industries tend to have a dominant player(s). Around 65 percent of the global tire market is dominated by four manufacturers. Fifty two percent of all ice cream sold in the United States is either chocolate, cookie flavor, or vanilla. The next 1,000 flavors don't add up to the top three.

Prime players are the dominant market player. They get attention because they are so dominant, so well known. Their strategic imperative is to defend against attention seekers and to acquire or assimilate emerging new threats created by authority businesses.

Each of the quads has a typical growth profile.

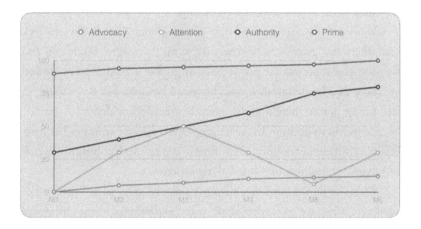

Advocacy has the slowest growth profile. It is predicated on the fact that building personal relationships takes time.

Attention businesses buy the attention of customers. In the digital world that is most often by way of purchased advertising, large retail presence, or search engine advertising.

In the digital world, attention is often purchased at the time a customer has the need and types their task into a search engine. When the advertising spend is reduced, we see an immediate effect on customer acquisition.

Typically, attention-based businesses don't gain a sustaining reputation beyond those who they have serviced well and conducted advocacy practices on to maintain the relationship.

Authority positions are attained by businesses practicing continued cycles of innovation, choosing their niche, and seeking to dominate and lead that niche by way of earned references from independent third parties.

Earned references include bloggers blogging about you and tweeters tweeting about your product, service, or cause. It can include magazines and industry commentators talking about your business. We cannot self-proclaim to be an industry authority. The true measure of an authority is underpinned by evidence of sustained, high volumes of peer-review attention for reasons of innovation or great storytelling.

It is through these references we build a brand reputation. Incredibly, once a reputation is gained, it carries with it a momentum that can last for a long time, unlike attention modeling.

Prime businesses are the industry giants. Depending on the lens lock used, the term "giant" can be a relative term. Remember Maddison and her pies? Her shop was the prime place for pies in a 1-mile radius around her shop. This is enough to sustain her retail business, but not enough to feed her ambition; therefore, she opens her lens lock wider.

She moves to become an authority player when we consider her marketability within her county. She's often asked to speak at business events and share her business-building baking experiences.

When she moves outside her county she falls to an overall position of advocacy. When we go further afield again, and we take in the entirety of the United States, her relationship with the entirety of the United States can only be described as "cold" (unlike her pies). Of 300 million plus people, only several thousand have any brand recognition.

For the sake of simple explanation, we'll take a large well-known global prime player, in this case Nike. Their marketing role, unlike rising authority businesses or attention businesses, is to be in a position of both defense and growth. They must defend from new innovators coming at them from the authority quadrant, and they must defend from brands in the attention quadrant wishing to out-advertise them.

It's easier for a prime brand to defend than for an authority or attention brand to attack. As shown with the tire and ice cream example, the major financial spoils go to the prime player. This leaves the prime player fully resourced to acquire or assimilate new innovative competitors and to out-spend rising attention brands.

An active prime brand like Nike will not be taken down by others out-spending them just as Coke wasn't displaced by Pepsi's spending. Once established, it is usually innovation that dislodges prime brands or their own internal inability to react to threats.

Here are the top five characteristics of each quad. The most effective way to establish the quadrant a business is in is to look at the supporting data. As we'll see in the next chapter, as the business moves from one quadrant to another so too does the website and social data profile.

Top Five Characteristics

Advocacy (or Word of Mouth)

1. Advocacy is the default starting position for businesses that have not taken deliberate action to invest in advertising, thus moving to attention or have not innovated to gain sustainable repeated references from industry publications and social influencers.
2. Data: Typically, advocacy businesses have a high percentage of website visits to their "people" page, "about us" page, or "contact us" page. This is because website readers are as interested in the people they're dealing with as the product/service they are purchasing.
3. Value proposition: Advocacy businesses often compete head-to-head with competitors' nondifferentiated value propositions. The value they proclaim to offer customers is usually based on "soft" points of difference anyone can claim. For example, "we have the best people."
4. Customers are typically obtained by offline efforts supported by digital marketing.
5. The marketing tactics that tend to be most successful are e-mail marketing and the managing of existing clients through social media interactions. An advocacy website focuses on the people within the company as much as the product or service it sells.

Authority (or Thought Leader)

Being good is not the same as being a thought leader. Most business leaders will claim "we're an industry authority." Unless they can produce evidence that they are publishing high-quality insights that are being shared by independent third parties, then it's likely they are simply "good at what they do," but not an industry authority. There is typically only room for a couple of industry authorities for any niche, no matter what the size the niche is.

Below are the top five characteristics of an authority business:

1. Authority businesses are those that have deliberately set out to lead a defined niche market and in doing so gain momentum, build brand equity, and gather customers by independent industry pundits referencing them. They typically publish their innovations and gain a reputation as a good source of industry insight.

2. Data: A typical profile of website traffic for an emerging authority business shows that most traffic comes from referral traffic and third party social shares. Over time "organic search" will increase as the brand starts to dominate the position of authority.

	Acquisition		
	Visits	↓ % New Visits	New Visits
	18,541	67.73%	12,557
Social	9,387		
Direct	2,798		
Referral	2,653		
Organic Search	2,083		
Email	921		
(Other)	699		

3. Value proposition: Most authority businesses are first to create a new or define an emerging market with a unique and clearly differentiated proposition to that of the current status quo.

4. Customers follow thought leaders. They share interest in the innovation, cause, or community that the authority business has created.

5. The marketing tactics that tend to be most successful are online Public Relations (PR), blogging, and YouTube channels that gain lots of subscriptions. Simply having these features on a website does not make an authority business. Content must be successfully syndicated and spread thereafter.

Attention (or Advertising Driven Business)

The advantage of running an attention-driven business is that demand can be created almost instantly. Once a website has been created, it takes little in the way of effort to set up online ads that target the desired audience.

The disadvantage of running an attention-driven business is that the cost of advertising is driven by auctioning search terms. It's not uncommon that the cost of advertising escalates over time until it equals or exceeds the value of the transaction. Retailers can spend $100 to get $75 in profit in the hope to retain a client for further transactions. Other kinds of businesses such as complex solution providers can spend thousands of dollars in the hope of gaining a new client. The running costs of this model can quickly get out of control. Once hooked on gaining clients using this method, it becomes a challenge to wean a business off this form of sales lead generation.

Below are the top five characteristics of an attention business:

1. Attention-driven businesses are the obvious choice for businesses that want to seek new customers via digital channels. It suits businesses that don't wish to change their offline business model to compete better online. Unlike authority businesses this kind of activity typically doesn't build brand equity as it simply responds to customer need rather than defining a market. As soon as the advertising stops, so too does the flow of new clients.

2. Data: Typically, attention-driven businesses see the clear majority of their website traffic coming from paid search.

3. Value proposition: Attention businesses often win business based on small points of differentiation or price. Rarely do attention-driven businesses have a "unique" value proposition.

4. New customers typically find the business from searching the web at their time of need.

5. The marketing tactics are search engine marketing, search engine optimization, and display advertising. The website of an attention-driven business focuses upon product features and price. It's common that a searcher bypasses the home page of attention-driven businesses as search engines and ad campaigns land them directly on the page that best answers the searchers query. Websites should be designed bearing this in mind.

Prime (The Dominant Industry Player)

This is the ultimate destination for any business, to become a dominant market player with a large percentage of market share.

The prime player has the great advantage over smaller businesses in that when it announces a new product or service, the industry often just assimilates and accepts the wishes of the prime. There is usually room for two or three prime players, and as such they typically obsess over retaining market share and defending against other prime players attacking their position. More often prime players can be blindsided not by other prime businesses but by rising authorities. For this reason, the three most important functions of a prime business are to innovate, defend against innovators, and spend cash on advertising to protect against attackers coming up from a position of attention.

Below are the top five characteristics of a prime business:

1. Prime position is not achieved or defined by a set of actions. It's the ultimate destination, the winner's podium for the largest businesses in any lens locked market. A business may be the prime player in one state, but if we widen the geography to include the entire country, the prime business can be dethroned by larger national businesses in this wider context.

2. Data: Typically, prime businesses gain the vast majority of their website traffic from people searching for them by their brand name. As the industry leader, most get large volumes of search engine or direct traffic.

3. Value proposition: The prime player often defines the entire market. They have a unique value proposition often achieved by way of having disproportionate resources to the competition.

4. New customers are typically drawn to the prime player based on reputation.

5. The prime player must acquire authority businesses that threaten its status or give it leverage into extending its market position. It defends against attention-driven businesses. Therefore, almost all digital marketing tactics are required depending on the scenario confronting a prime player in any situation. A prime website should be designed to reduce customer inertia and allow them to complete their task as swiftly as possible. Unlike authority websites, the prime player doesn't have to convince readers of its credentials, and therefore, blogging and other authority tactics are not necessary to maintain position.

CHAPTER 7

The Sixth Principle of Digital Business Strategy— Engine of Growth

As we've seen in the previous chapter, once we establish our "lens lock" we can use a combination of website analytics and business characteristics to plot where our business is at any moment in time on the Ionology quadrant. Once we've established where we are, we can decide where we would like to be. The ultimate destination is to hold the prime position in our chosen market.

There are a few additional rules regarding the quadrant. It's not possible to be in more than one position on the quadrant at any one time. A classified ads business can have two sets of customers: the advertisers and readers. While they both require the same product, their needs are very different, and therefore, the business may require two separate strategies for dealing with each customer type resulting in two separate strategy boards.

It's not possible to be in between two plot points. We must start at one position on the quadrant and choose to either enhance the position we're at or move position to a different point. As we'll see in the next chapter, the path between two points on the quadrant is plotted by laying out the major steps that should be taken to reach the destination.

Most organizations can claim primacy if they adjust the lens lock to match their strengths. Let's look at an example: Majestic Fruit and Vegetable Distribution is the prime player in their home city as they distribute over 40 percent of all fresh fruit to hotels and restaurants in their locality. Should their ambition be to simply maintain their position, then they need to continuously innovate and improve to keep out competition from more advanced players while maintaining their local advertising and sponsorship activity. However, should they change their lens lock and decide that they want to become a major player within their state, not just within their local city, they soon find that they are no longer a "prime" business. In fact, their distribution covers less than 5 percent of the market when we look at the entire state and we soon run into much larger better established businesses that have more resources.

The neighboring city has a smattering of small local distribution businesses that Majestic would consider as being microbusinesses (so small as to be incidental). It would also have city-specific suppliers who have grown up over time to be similar in size and ability to Majestic. There are also national competitors. These are large multinational suppliers. They tend to supply the large hotel and restaurant chains and aren't that interested in the small independents. Majestic is too small to even consider going for a national hotel or restaurant chain like Hilton or Hard Rock Café. It sees its target market as the independent restaurant or small owner-run hotel chains.

Before Majestic can define its move on the Ionology quadrant it must add perspective. In Principle 1, know yourself, we ask that a business state its strategic ambition.

YOURSELF   1

Diagnosis

While we would like to grow from a city supplier of fresh fruit and vegetables, we have yet to find an innovation that would differentiate us sufficiently to give reason for customers to wish to migrate.

Strategic Ambition

To grow our state wide marketshare by out-innovating our largest competitor and capturing the majority of wholesale fruit market in the hospitality sector.

Unique Value Proposition

At this stage, it is unknown

In this situation, Majestic has a desire for growth but can see that without a unique value proposition powered by an innovation its options are limited. In essence, they are performing an attack on an incumbent supplier who should not be underestimated because they are good at what they do, they are well managed, and they are well resourced.

At this moment of planning, when looking at becoming a statewide distributor leveraging its single city foothold, Majestic can be concluded as a niche player because it services a single market within a single city. It has three engines of growth options:

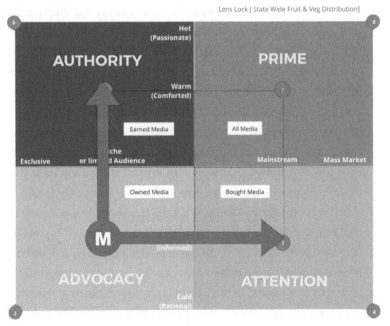

Option 1: Grow via advocacy, Option 2: grow via attention, Option 3: grow via authority

An overview of each move:

1. *Try to grow via advocacy.* That is to try and expand its sales team and build new relationships with new restaurants and hotels in new areas outside of the city limits it currently operates in. The challenge with this kind of growth is that existing suppliers are already operating in this area and if anything Majestic is disadvantaged as their goods must be

shipped further from the distribution center than local suppliers. Staying in advocacy is going to be a long hard slog if they are to gain market share in what are already well-serviced new territories. In fact, striving for growth in this way is likely to bring a risk to Majestic as the only obvious lever available to the business on which to base its beachhead in new territories is to reduce its prices and effectively start a price war.

2. *Move from advocacy to attention*: A second option open to Majestic is to deploy an attention-based marketing program to try to pick up disgruntled customers or new start businesses that pop up in the newly expanded territory they plan to service. They consider sponsoring a golf tournament in the new territory but discover that this tactic has been established by their competitors and is in its 20th year. They look to spend money on trade advertising but find it difficult to justify the money spent as their competitors are already established and doing the same. They look to find sales opportunities using SEO optimization, but when they look at the activities of their competitors, they realize that this is already a heavily contested space and shifting a competitor from a natural search engine position could be almost impossible. The same challenge applies to paid search; the cost of acquiring a new customer is prohibitively high.

3. *Move from advocacy to authority*: While this may seem like the only option available to Majestic, it is the hardest to execute because it presumes that the business can transform itself through innovation and present a new alternative proposition to the marketplace. As we know, being an authority is measured by the outcome that our business is referenced frequently for the innovations we provide by industry publications and experts. To achieve this outcome, Majestic will have to divert much of its profits into creating a sequence of new industry changing innovations in order to gain such recognition. As a third-generation family-owned wholesale business, they prefer to modernize over time than to radically innovate in order to go grow. Innovation simply isn't within their DNA.

How Majestic Got to Where it is Today

Majestic is a 35-year-old business. If we lens lock our view on their home city, we can see how the business has grown over this time. In the early days, it was unknown and the founders had to establish their credentials with a few trusting clients. It grew slowly, built a good reputation, serviced their clients well, and acquired one customer at a time principally by the founder knocking doors day after day and asking for business. Once the business started to accumulate profits, it started to advertise to build brand recognition with unfamiliar customers. The sales force grew and account managers were charged with delivering a quality service to their existing customers as well as seeking new customers.

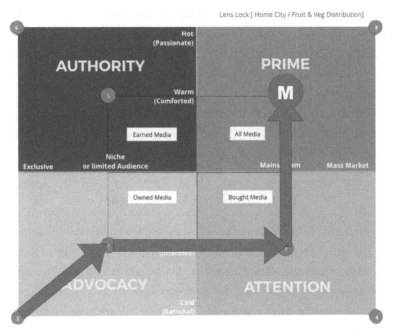

Majestic's 35-year journey in its home city

The business continued to grow by repeating its marketing formula over and over: buying ads, sponsoring events, and servicing customers to the best of their ability. They maintained their advocacy activity as they moved to attention. They discovered that "bought media" helped account managers win new customers and it gave comfort to existing customers that they had chosen the right supplier.

Over the last 20 years, the business has acquired several smaller competitors and expanded its range into more exotic fruit and vegetables as well as prepared foods. Its logistics center has grown, it now has a telesales team and an e-commerce website, and of course it still maintains its account executives' weekly customer visits. Within its own city and logistic limits, Majestic has slowly grinded out a position of primacy.

As the second generation of family owners matures, however, they want to reset the lens lock and grow the business further throughout the state. The market is different now than it was 35 years ago when the original founders started. There weren't any national competitors back then. Logistics were simpler, customers were less demanding, and there was a more willing acceptance to try the "new local guy" based on reputation.

If Majestic was to expand into several cities, it didn't want to take another 35 years to do so. They didn't have enough cash to acquire and assimilate competitors and getting in the door of what are already well-serviced customers was going to be a challenge for even the most experienced account executives.

Faced with these three potential strategic business moves, the senior management team within Majestic considers the consequences of each move along with the actions and challenges they'll face.

Trying to Grow Via Advocacy

We know that Majestic started off with a strong sales ethic and built a brand by spending wisely on advertising and brand promotion. It grew into a position of strength within its native city by servicing owner-managed restaurants, hotels, and small hotel groups. It now has a desire to grow into surrounding cities and would like to have a marketing-led strategy that would enable this growth.

An abbreviated version of its strategy could be written as follows:

Know Yourself

Diagnosis: The company has desires to grow into other geographic markets but hasn't yet established a point of differentiation. It hopes to leverage its long track record of good customer support, but it doesn't yet know if that's enough to gain market share.

Strategic ambition: To grow organically to become a prime statewide supplier of fruit and vegetables to its target audience within the next 5 years.

Unique value proposition: We are the state's longest established providers of fruit and vegetables to small and medium restaurants and hotels.

Each of the above makes for a poor strategy.

The diagnosis is based on a leap of faith assumption that customers can be gained by simply replicating practices that have worked in Majestic's home city for 35 years, elsewhere.

The strategic ambition assumes that competitors can be outperformed and customers persuaded to change supplier especially to an "unknown" supplier like Majestic who have no track record beyond their own home city.

The unique value proposition assumes customers want to seek a new supplier that has been established for several years in another city. It's hard to see how this proposition actually offers any value to the customer.

Know Your Customer

Volume: Using a Google Adwords tool entitled "Keyword Planner," Majestic has found that there are over 100 searches per month in their state for people seeking "wholesale fruit" or "wholesale vegetables." They believe that this shows there is demand beyond their own city for a new supplier.

Task: Unknown

Intent: Unknown

While they know the volume of search engine activity in their target state, they don't know the *task* of the searcher when they type these keywords into their search engine. Are they looking for a supplier of wholesale fruit and vegetables or could it be that they are home users wanting to find out if they can get low-cost food online? Moreover, search volume doesn't tell us the *intent* of the searcher. Assuming 20 percent of the searchers are from independent restaurant owners and hoteliers, are they seeking to purchase fruit and vegetables? Is their intent to switch supplier or are they simply looking to price check?

Until these major assumptions are validated, these data are all but useless. The marketing leaders within Majestic must run experiments to understand if there really is statewide demand for another wholesaler in this market. Rather than rush to create test websites, the leadership suggests that this is a major mile marker that must be understood and so they place it into the strategy execution section of the strategy board (Principle 7, strategy execution).

The business knows the volume of people searching online for wholesale goods, but it doesn't know if it's their target market, and if it is their target market, what will make them switch to a new supplier. Answering these kind of unknowns is a primary task of any marketer and as we will see, something that can be completed rapidly. How they find the relevant data is not for debate during strategy meetings, only that it must be found.

Next the business leaders need to look at the competition they must either displace or outflank.

Competition

Competitors: They are numerous and better established and some have access to greater resources than Majestic.

Proposition: Each of the competitors has their own website and each claims to have the biggest, fastest, freshest, and widest selection of goods. They all claim to offer the best service and they all want to become "your supplier of choice."

Force: Force is a calculable number. It's a combination of the size of the company in any particular market and how actively they are marketing. The mass of an organization is simply a measurement of their turnover as a percentage measured against other competitors. If the turnover of the largest competitor is $10,000,000 and the second business has a turnover of $5,000,000, the first business has a mass of 100 and the second has a mass of 50.

Acceleration is a measurement of how digitally active a business is. This can be obtained from Ionology.com/dmd/. The number is generated by checking out the frequency content is produced, the number of inbound links, and how many people are citing the business for its innovations.

A business with a large turnover but with low activity can theoretically be displaced by a smaller business that's much more active. A large business that retains a prime position in Majestic's target market will be hard to displace even if their marketing activity is much less than that of Majestic. A large mass with low momentum is very difficult to shift using attention-based techniques.

The only real way to shift a larger prime player in a new market when you have lower resources is to out-innovate them.

Resources

Time: The time required to operate an advocacy model is high. It typically requires a marketer to prepare print marketing materials to support sales representatives and create e-mail marketing campaigns to target existing customers and new sales opportunities gained by the sales team. Time is often spent on social media although engagement is low due to the lack of having something innovative or unique to say.

Talent: The term "talent" refers to leadership talent. This is often not present in an advocacy approach. The organizational leadership usually let the marketing team get on with their job and there's little in the way of interference.

Cash: There is a low cash requirement as most of the marketing collateral is distributed to existing customers by the sales force as well as via e-mail and social media.

Advocacy Summary

In conclusion, this strategy is perceived to be the lowest risk model as it simply extends the operational functions of the current business and attempts to step-and-repeat the actions they have perfected over years of being in business within their own city limits.

The reality is that this is not a marketing-led strategy; it's a sales-led plan. They defend their current position in their home city where they are well known and respected. To grow statewide and deploy these same actions assume that this model will work. It's not certain whether it will, but if it does work growth will be extremely slow.

The risk to the business is that they lose focus on their local market if they extend themselves into the new market.

Trying to Grow by Attention

When trying to grow a business via attention, it's not unusual that the business first establishes its ability to carry out an advocacy model. This means that they have base technology and marketing requirements fulfilled. They effectively use Customer Relationship Management (CRM) tools as well as e-mail marketing and social media. They typically have low volumes of social media members and e-mails are typically only well received when they there are sent to customers that wish to receive them.

Attention modeling is simply buying the attention of customers interested in a product or service. This usually means paid advertising on search engines, display ads, and sponsorship. Any marketing activity where there is a direct cost of sale associated with obtaining the customer is said to be part of an attention plan.

Obtaining customers via attention modeling requires a different kind of website than using advocacy modeling. In advocacy, the customer finds the website because of the marketing efforts of the sales force and the internal sales team. As advocacy is all about supporting other sales efforts that are going on, customers tend to use the advocacy website to look up more information on the person coming to visit them, the history of the company, and who else is using the company. Advocacy websites should be built to highlight the people within the organization.

When it comes to attention modeling, the customer tends to have a completely different priority. They are online to perform a task. When they are searching for "wholesale fruit," they typically want to see the price of wholesale fruit and vegetables. They are less interested in the sales representatives and account managers. They want to answer their own questions first before they'll be interested in finding out about the people within the organization. For this reason, attention models favor e-commerce style websites. They are often built to elicit the best search engine results and help the searcher complete the task they came to do.

This is why it's difficult to have an advocacy plan and an attention plan at the same time. The same content, marketing activity, and website design should not be used.

When creating the advocacy strategy Majestic found they were missing some key pieces of information. They hoped to pick up new customers via digital marketing and used information from Google Adwords to show that there was indeed demand for their services statewide. What they didn't know was if the customer was looking for the price of wholesale fruit and vegetables or if they wanted to change supplier. To obtain this information, they needed to run an experiment. Attention modeling is the way in which experiments are conducted.

The challenge most organizations like Majestic face before they choose an advocacy or attention model is that they need to know the customer task and intent. They don't want to create an advocacy website if they need an e-commerce website and they don't want to make an attention-driven e-commerce website if customers don't want to use it. The solution to this conundrum is to build a temporary website from a template and test the proposition.

There are many locations on the web where a marketer can purchase an e-commerce template, rapidly stock it with products, and link it to a shopping basket. The marketer should populate the website with outrageously low-cost products and then purchase search engine ads. The marketer may not even use the brand of their own company for the experiment.

The purpose of the experiment is to find out if an attention model was deployed and we had the lowest cost product on the market, would our unfamiliar brand be able to attract customers and what would it cost to acquire these customers.

Most businesses can take this kind of testing approach. Within 3 days, a website and ad campaign can be up and running and within 2 weeks an abundance of data gathered to see if attention modeling will work. If it does and the business is able to acquire customers, even at a loss, it means that we at least know the "Task" that customers were trying to perform and that their "Intent" to was purchase.

The business now has a choice. Does it run an attention model that leads the sales operation in attracting new customers or does it run a pure advocacy model where the digital marketing supports the sales representative's efforts rather than leads them.

The resource requirements for an attention model are different from that of an advocacy model. With an attention model "Cash" is often the defining parameter as the marketing "Time" is usually quite low once things are up and running and leadership "Talent" isn't needed.

An attention model requires a different kind of marketer than that of advocacy modeling. The advocacy model requires a marketer capable of creating cohesion between the business, its sales force, and the customer. An attention model requires that the marketer uses data to find the lowest cost of acquisition, to displace competitors, and to win the battle of the search engines. An attention model requires much more scientific analysis of data, while the advocacy marketer requires much more empathy with the customer and sales force.

Attention Summary

This experimentation technique can be used to validate assumptions. It can also be used to run a profitable e-commerce business assuming competitors can be displaced, customers can be won, and the cost of acquisition is at a profitable, sustainable level.

The challenge many attention-driven strategies have is that the cost of acquisition of a new customer is not static. While it can be profitable one week, the next week a new competitor can push the cost of acquisition up in paid advertising and displace the business from its coveted natural search engine position.

Move to Authority

As mentioned in the previous chapter, becoming an authority requires earning media coverage, inbound links, and social media shares due to repeated innovation. While most businesses claim to be innovative, they are actually creative. They rarely have a sustainable program of innovation designed to differentiate them within the marketplace or indeed change the market.

The new young leaders of Majestic, however, are keen to explore this avenue. They investigate many methods of creating innovative concepts in a sustainable way. The on-trend method of innovation planning is Design School (D-School) thinking from Stanford University. The leadership team meets to explore if they can reinvent products and services to help them get into their expanded marketplace with a more unique offering.

In the Seven Principles of Digital Business Strategy they return to Principle 1—Diagnosis. This section of Principle 1 demands that we truly understand the customer's challenge(s) and make our product and services to solve those challenges.

Mark is the youngest leader of Majestic; he invites several customers from their existing client base in for a hosted session of D-School innovation. They soon discover that their customers have different challenges from those they thought they had.

The current Majestic service delivers fruit and vegetables in the morning to allow chefs to prepare food for the day ahead. What Majestic's customers explained during the innovation session was that many of the more delicate fruits and vegetables were starting to wither by the evening forcing them to put them into refrigeration. The fridge was taking up valuable real estate within the kitchen and they felt that more frequent deliveries, perhaps two times per day would allow them to reduce the amount of refrigeration they needed.

They also complained that they found themselves short of key ingredients and found it difficult to order the exact quantities of products leading to wastage.

If Majestic was to deliver further away from its base it couldn't offer more frequent deliveries for a variety of reasons including fleet availability, parking, and unloading restrictions and the need for new distribution centers.

As the innovation process continued, they understood that customers would find it very convenient if they could order key ingredients with 2 hours' notice and have the goods delivered fresh to their kitchens. This could in essence allow them to regain valuable floor space and have fresh produce with key ingredients available within 2 hours 24/7.

Mark and his team looked at new pedal bike delivery methods, chilled storage using liquid nitrogen, and small local warehousing. They felt that a model of having key ingredients delivered and refrigerated at key locations around their target cities with rapid bike delivery would allow them to not only differentiate themselves but also charge a premium for the goods.

They set to work trialing this method by first creating a brochure that explained the service. The brochure contained some stock photography, illustrations, and photos of the team at Majestic. When the sales force presented this concept at the opening meeting with their new potential clients in the nearby city, they found that the customer was immediately receptive to the concept and wanted to know more. Before having this brochure, they found that potential customers were reluctant to engage. They claimed they already had a supplier who met their needs.

For Majestic, this was their first encounter with game changing innovation. It didn't take them long to realize that if this gets them "in the door" with new customers, all they had to do was to continuously innovate to differentiate themselves and use these innovations as the small end of the wedge. Their investment in trialing these innovations was small at first and leveraged the assets within the business to allow them to modify their existing service and enhance the customer experience.

These innovations made marketing Majestic easy. They now had a unique value proposition. They were now the only supplier able to offer 2-hour delivery 24/7. As the uptake of the service was generally low, yet the impact in terms of a differentiated message was high, the firm was able to recruit a small army of willing cyclists to take the chilled packages on the back of their bikes from a small regional refrigeration unit on the outskirts of town when an order came in via their mobile app.

Leading innovation like this is a great way to get industry attention. A press release and a few interviews later, Majestic was able to proclaim that they were expanding offering a unique service, superior to all other suppliers. By the time their competitors were even contemplating what was going on, Majestic was already on to their second innovation. Disposal of waste where they carried the cost of the disposal!

The design of an authority website is different from that of an attention or advocacy website. It is usually built around the unique value proposition. The technology featured on the home page was the 2-hour delivery 24/7 mobile app. The app allowed for ordering of key high-demand items and nothing else. It was a simple solution at first that became more feature rich as time went on.

Creating an authority play demands that the leadership talent is heavily involved. It can also consume a lot of marketing time but very little cash, in terms of resource used. Good innovations tend to travel quickly through social media and peer review publications.

Majestic has stuck with their processes of constant innovation and are now progressing their 3-year plan of authority, upending entrenched competitors by changing customer expectations. They are growing rapidly and are currently looking at powering their own factory from organic waste collected by cyclists and returning delivery vehicles.

Authority Summary

This is the hardest to execute although it brings a wealth of benefit. As we've seen in the previous chapter, authority businesses get a disproportionate amount of attention from those businesses that conduct attention and advocacy strategies. Their website needs a blog and relies on the distribution of stories regarding the innovations of the business. The true measure of the success of the innovation is how well the concept is received by customers and the industry media.

The real challenge for the marketer in this case is coming up with a constant stream of new stories of how the innovation changed peoples' lives within the industry. Telling a human story can often seem like it's not helping the business achieve its goals, but human stories travel much better than stories about advancing technology or work practices.

The leadership must remain involved and committed to creating cycles of continuous sustaining innovations if the marketing is to work and the business is to become an industry authority.

Once an authority position is achieved, the corporate ambition can shift to becoming the prime business within the defined lens lock. This is often achieved by simply innovating, innovating, and innovating again. At some point, the existing prime business will look to acquire the emerging authority, but if momentum favors the authority, they may eventually swallow the prime!

CHAPTER 8

The Fourth Principle of Digital Business Strategy— Resources

As promised at the beginning of Chapter 6, we now return to our Fourth Principle. In practical terms, when you are creating a digital business strategy you can of course work through the principles in sequential order and look at resources after Principles 1, 2, and 3. Resources and engine of growth are so closely intertwined, that resources can end up determining which engines of growth are available as will shortly become clear.

Many businesses begin formulating their strategy from the point of ambition, which they pinpoint under the "Know Yourself" principle. They look at what they would like to achieve, and they set out how to achieve it through their strategy. Other businesses approach their strategy from the perspective of "Know Your Customer"; they look at what their customers wish to achieve and tailor their strategy around that in the hope that it will positively affect the business. Yet other businesses approach strategy from a marketplace perspective, spotting opportunities and gaps in the market and creating strategies that aim to fill those gaps and take those opportunities. Finally, some (though fewer) businesses begin with resources. Resources, and their breakdown into time, talent, and cash, are reflected heavily in the engine of growth and often restrict or dictate which plays are available to us when we wish to move from one position to another.

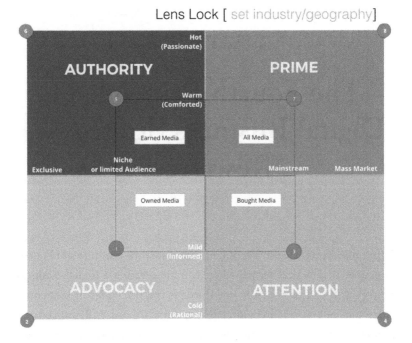

In terms of resources, we find that advocacy requires time. This tends to be those skilled in marketing that will take time to perform tasks like e-mail marketing, delivering content to existing customers, and running their own social media channels.

If we look at businesses that wish to have rapid growth and have existing customer demand, and space in the marketplace that has not been flooded out by competitors, the resource that they most need is cash. This will allow them to purchase advertising and other means to attain customer attention in a profitable way that allows for business growth.

If we manage to move above the X-axis, we can gain more attention for our business. We have moved into the position of an authority or of a prime player in the marketplace. To become an authority player, the resource that we need is talent. We must circulate our story and make it travel within the niche that we are servicing. This requires creative talents: story writing, playwriting, poetry, and so on. We need the talents of those who are able to create narratives that spread. This spreading of narrative, if we aim to become an authority, is of utmost importance, since we cannot declare ourselves an authority—we can only be declared so by the wider industry, by way of them referencing us through social media and their own published articles. More often than not, the type of attention that allows us to rise above the X-axis is earned through innovation that is evidenced by way of ever-increasing referral traffic coming from relevant third-party sites. These empirical, analytics-based characteristics are the defining measurement of an authority business. Many businesses may declare themselves "authorities" in their own world, but without evidence they can't declare it in a digital world.

Prime businesses are usually in a defensive position. They are looking out for authority businesses who are trying to come into the more mainstream market, and for people coming up across the X-axis from attention. They require all three resources—time, talent, and cash, but usually have these resources in abundance because they are, after all, the prime player.

The question then is: which of these moves are going to be best for your business?

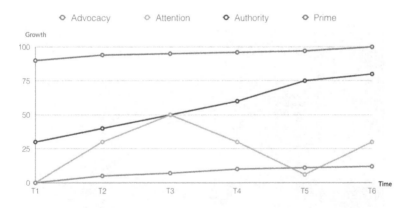

Typical Business Growth Profiles

This chart shows the typical growth profiles associated with each engine of growth in the Ionology quadrant.

As we have mentioned, there is no "bad" quadrant. Advocacy has the slowest growth, attention requires cash, and becoming an authority and moving above the X-axis can be extremely difficult. Usually only two or three businesses get there for any given subniche. Even so, we ought to consistently aim to increase our brand warmth and move above the X-axis. A business above the X-axis gains substantially more traffic than those below. Few make it, but all roads should try to lead to authority or prime. Even if we do not succeed in becoming an authority or a prime player, the higher we are on the X-axis, the more growth we can expect. Of course, if we do manage to push our business above the X-axis and become an authority or a prime player, it becomes very difficult for competitors to attack us from below unless a competing business has a huge amount of cash resources or they have an industry-changing innovation.

Businesses who have diagnosed their current position (as detailed in Chapter 6) will always be trying to move upward on the quadrant—and if at all possible, to move to the right. For any business, there are a defined number of plays available to them. Moving from a cold rational exclusive business, for example, up to becoming a mainstream, mild, informed business or niche business, requires a certain set of steps and plays. Each of these steps usually requires a change in website, value proposition, and customer base. It means figuring out what we need to do to create the stories, news, and brand warmth that will help us with targeting new customers. The business must decide which play(s) it wants to make, based upon what resources it has at hand, what innovation it has, and what cash it has available.

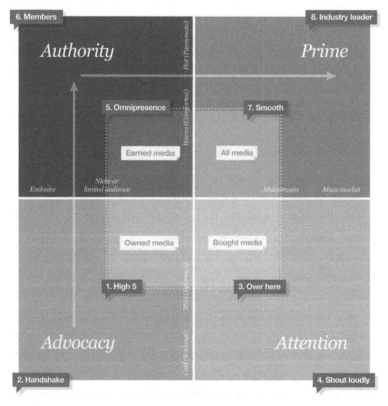

The Ionology quadrant

Not all businesses are going to win in the digital context. As we know, the positions in the inner square of the quadrant have much better results in dealing with digital and using digital for promotion than the outer square. In positions 2 and 4, where we're down at cold and rational, we usually don't need social media. Social media have practically no part to play from a tactical standpoint, because the only reason the customer wants to communicate with businesses in position 4 is to complain about a failed product or service.

When we move up from position 4 into being a mild and informed business, then social media—our own social media—become important to us. If we move up further to positions 5 and 7, earned media and social media become extremely important. Choosing the right tactics and the way that we execute those tactics will depend upon where we are right now and where we are going to go.

We tend to find ourselves in positions 4 and 8, at the right-hand side of the quadrant when we're in mass markets. In this situation engagement in social media and the like can become too overwhelming, engagement solves no business objective, or the customer has no desire to "follow their favorite brand of bleach." In other words, there is simply too little return for our efforts.

The inner square, then, is where the digital opportunity lies, and that is where we're aiming to get to if we want to build a digital business, and we want to use digital as a promotional tool effectively and efficiently.

For these engines of growth, we have given each starting position a name as a reflection of how digital translates into the being of the business. The names are as follows:

Position 1: High Five

A business in advocacy in the inner quadrant is using digital to service its customers. E-mail marketing and the business' own social media are driving traffic to their website.

Position 2: Handshake

Most traditional businesses are in position 2. They are in advocacy and they do not actively use digital to gain new customers. In business-to-business industries new business is sought through a sales team on the road with a basic online presence of a brochure-type website with the "contact us" and "about us" pages being the most highly trafficked.

Position 3: Over Here! Over Here!

This type of business uses paid-for digital tactics to gain attention. The suite of tactics includes pay-per-click, display advertising and remarketing as well as their own media—social, e-mail newsletters, and price-based offers, to drive traffic to their website.

Position 4: Shout Loudly

Similar to position 3, shout loudly also dictates that a business must additionally use offline tactics for brand building, while the website and online presence are primarily used for servicing demand.

Position 5: Omnipresent

This business needs to be everywhere; speaking at events and hosting webinars. They need to have a content engine creating written and video content for training, blogs, and PR, which are featured in influential publications and shared on other people's social media—as opposed to their own social media. Digital tools include enterprise resource planning (ERP) and customer relationship management (CRM) systems to manage customers. New customers are drawn to the business as influencers are talking about the business as an authority.

Position 6: Members

This business is a very elite one that only wishes to talk to those who are also in the elite group. This position is an authority but does not use digital as a sales tool. Client support tends to be the digital play at hand.

Position 7: Smooth

For this business, demand is not the challenge—servicing demand is. In a prime spot, servicing the demand through a highly effective website becomes the best area of focus. The business in prime position uses all digital media tools; advocacy tactics to retain its loyal customers, innovation to gain new customers, and attention tactics to defend their position.

Position 8: Hot Leader

For businesses in this position, continued innovation is most important if we are to stay in position as the hot leader and get additional traffic and higher margins. Traditional media including television, radio, and Outdoor advertising all have an important role in maintaining this position.

We must be careful, in looking at our engine of growth and formulating our strategies, that we do not credit the syringe, rather than the medicine, for fixing the problem. Quite often, a business will perform a tactic, say, e-mail marketing, and when it's successful they will think that the delivery method has brought them success, when in fact it was the content *delivered* that has brought them success. The content is the medicine, and the syringe can only be effective at curing the problem if the correct medicine is used. In the world of marketing, we must always focus on content and ensure that it conveys our unique value proposition in a way that will attract customers to do business with us. To look at our internal analysis then, we must ensure that our content conveys our value proposition, meets a need for the customer, stands out in the marketplace, and can be delivered within the confines of our available resources.

For businesses in advocacy, the tactics tend to be e-mail marketing, our own social media, search, and a CRM system. Businesses in the attention part of the quadrant tend to use paid search, natural search, display advertising, and e-mail marketing to maintain customers once they have them. Businesses sitting in the authority quadrant usually need to focus on the creation of good-quality content, and spread it online, both through their own avenues and through other businesses and consumers sharing their content. Being an authority involves connecting with others to allow them to share your good knowledge and maintain your visibility as an authority figure in your given niche. For prime players, business is all about delivering on-demand, good usability, self-service, and defending the channels of attack coming from authority and from attention. Additionally, prime businesses must always keep a focus on innovation.

Even though these tactics are recommended and most frequently successfully used in strategic terms for the various locations on the quadrant, none of them are mutually exclusive. It doesn't mean that prime players don't get involved in e-mail marketing, for example. Of course they do, but the tactics described above are the top tactical responses required for each starting position. As the position of a business on the quadrant changes, so will the priority of different tactics.

Similarly, there are different types of websites required, dependent upon what move we wish to make. Businesses in advocacy often find that new customers are looking at information about their people more than any other part of their website. They have come to the website because of a personal recommendation so they already know what the company does but want to find out more about the people and services, which is evidenced in the website analytics. For a business in a position of authority, the reason new customers arrive on their website is because of news of their innovation, and so it's important that authority business' websites aptly showcase their innovation front and center, so the new customers know they have come to the right place. An authority website should also be content-driven and designed in a way that encourages sharing and syndication of the content. Businesses in the attention part of the quadrant are focused on the four Ps of marketing, namely product, price, place, and promotion. They must present their proposition to the customer in the right way to gain their business. Finally, a company in the prime part of the quadrant will need to focus its efforts on understanding process to ensure that they have a website that is efficient and user-friendly for servicing its large customer base. In large organizations, there is also a huge challenge in presenting the vast hierarchy of products and services that cover all the divisions and business units that make up the organization. The internal wrangling and politics may lead to a confusing website as each business division strives to have their product or service showcased—but it is the tasks that the customer is trying to achieve that must take priority.

We must always keep in mind that our position on the quadrant can and will change, and we must always be prepared to reevaluate and redesign our strategy if and when the position changes. Before we make a move it's important that we have the right baseline and base camp. Baseline is made up of figures and statistics: where are we now and how many customers are coming to us by different channels. The important channels to analyze are social, referral, and direct traffic. Base camp is about getting the right tools that enable us to make the move we have decided upon. If we're going to move from advocacy to attention, we need to make sure we have the right people, with the right training and skills to understand the science of display advertising, pay-per-click advertising, remarketing, and SEO. If, on the other hand, we are staying in advocacy, we need to be sure we have the right e-mail marketing tools and the ability to create content that resonates with customers. This content may also change over time, dependent upon our strategic desires.

Assuming we have our baseline figures, and we have our base camp set up with all the right tools, we can then make the move we have selected. For the purpose of this book, we're going to use the journey north from advocacy to authority. This is the most frequently desired journey, but not the most frequently travelled. The most frequently travelled is from advocacy to attention where businesses build a website, put up ads, and hope to attain new customers. As discussed earlier, though, the biggest increase in customers, and consequently growth, comes when a business builds brand warmth.

So how do you move from advocacy to authority?

Something counterintuitive must happen first. Quite often, businesses look at the market and build a value proposition that is too generic; they're servicing the customer in the same way as hundreds, if not thousands, of other businesses. The key here is to find a unique value proposition, rather than a generic one, and to focus upon that. That unique value proposition is all the business should care to talk about. The reason this is counterintuitive is because most businesses feel they will exclude many opportunities that could come their way by having such a narrow focus. The reality is that when we build our business around the niche that we're trying to service within our lens lock, we gain more customers because we're perceived to be the best at what we do.

The other reason we need to keep our focus so narrow is because it takes us a tremendous amount of energy to move from advocacy to authority. Imagine attempting to blow a ping-pong ball upward across the X-axis of the quadrant. The wider the tube, the more breath—the more energy—we need to use. At a certain point, the tube becomes so wide that the task is impossible. The narrower the tube—the more pinpointed our niche—the more focused our energy is, and the more likely we are to succeed. Spreading the niche wider makes the customer perceive that you couldn't be an expert. It's not until a business becomes prime that it is perceived to be able to start off new Advocacy to authority journeys in different market sectors and still be believed to be able to deliver.

One of the other great benefits of keeping the niche narrow is that often the prime businesses don't view a small niche as worthy of their attention, because it doesn't affect their balance sheets enough.

Let's look at a company that everyone knows—a prime player in its field and an authority in yet more—Apple. How did Apple become an authority? How did they move into prime? And how did competitors handle it?

We know that moving up on the quadrant requires innovation, and we know that moving to attention and prime requires cash. When Steve Jobs rejoined Apple, the company had multiple products and multiple sectors; it was in the server market and the peripherals market and Jobs removed practically everything the company did. This wouldn't necessarily work for every business, but his first act was to declutter the business and start focusing on one thing, in other words, to pare down to a point of having a unique value proposition.

In 1998, the business built the first iMac computer. The first iMac was created by Jonathan Ive along with Steve Jobs, and it was a unique product to the marketplace. The advertising that went with this depicted an 8-year-old boy and his dog, Max. It showed Max and the boy getting their home computer connected through a modem that was built into the computer, and the slogan was "there is no step three." The advertisement went on to show a PhD student trying to use an IBM Windows personal computer to connect to the Internet, and the 8-year-old boy had done it before him. Jobs had narrowed the niche to home computer users who were looking to connect to the Internet. This was an emerging wave at the time.

Jobs' innovation was to make the simplest tool to allow the home Internet user to get online. The visual design helped, but what sold the product was keeping the niche narrow and understanding the customer— understanding the gap in the marketplace and filling it with innovation that propelled the business forward.

In 2001, Apple released iTunes, which was its second innovation; 8.5 months later, it released the iPod. The iPod opened to a crowd of around 50,000 people. Today, more people than that queue around the block at Apple stores when a new product is released. The iPod was not the first MP3 music player to market, but we know it was one of the best executed.

Next came the innovation of the iTunes store that revolutionized how we buy music, and in 2007, the iPhone was released followed by the iPad in 2010. Apple's retail and these innovations are all uniquely innovative and all defensible.

Inside the small niche of home computing and Internet access, Apple moved, through innovation, to become an authority. From there, they were able to expand their product portfolio.

Becoming a prime player in almost every field they entered, Apple began to cause disruption and displacement. They displaced Nokia as prime player for the mobile phone market through their innovations and through defending those innovations. Many businesses have tried to take on Apple in the mobile phone market, and many have failed. Other businesses tried to use their cash reserves to buy media in an attempt to move above the X-axis, from attention to prime. Apple's market position was so strong at this point, thanks to continued cycles of innovation and a hot brand reputation that all these attempts failed. Some businesses tried to innovate, but their innovations didn't appeal to customers or were not significantly innovative enough to draw customers away from the hot brand of Apple.

The only business that managed to join Apple as a prime player was Samsung. Samsung spent billions of dollars on attention and were eventually able to cross the X-axis of our quadrant to become a prime player. As a result, we're now seeing that Apple and Samsung are increasingly dominant in Europe and the United States. There are new approaches coming from the east, where there are other new players entering the market, but this is because the product life cycle is starting to reach its pinnacle and go downstream again.

From an article by Patrick Seitz, in the investor's business daily:

"Apple (AAPL) and Samsung continue to soak up all the industry's profits," McCourt says. "Apple claimed 87.4 percent of phone earnings before interest and taxes in the fourth quarter," he said. "Samsung took in 32.2 percent of industry profits. Because their combined earnings were higher than the industry's total earnings as a result of many vendors losing money in fourth quarter, Apple and Samsung mathematically accounted for more than 100 percent of the industry's earnings," Seitz reports. "A year ago, Apple accounted for 77.8 percent of mobile phone industry profits, followed by Samsung with 26.1 percent," McCourt said.

We can see that coming from attention to take on the prime players is extremely difficult unless you spend more cash than the prime players are spending. This explains why many businesses prefer to become an authority in a niche and move across to prime. If a business is in a marketplace where the incumbent in prime position is already executing highly innovative cycles, their best play may be to avoid the prime player's market niches and attempt to create a new one.

Not all businesses have what it takes to move above the X-axis on our quadrant, but for those that do, we can usually build a 10-point plan.

1. Focused Cycles of Deliberate Agile Innovation

To move upward on the quadrant, we must have deliberately designed, focused cycles of innovation, and that innovation must solve a challenge by creating a new market niche or displacing an authority that is already in that niche. Not all innovations need to be wholeheartedly industry disrupting, but those that do disrupt tend to move up to an authority position faster than those that are not disruptive. The creation of innovation is not an innovation unless the customer or the industry peers deem it to be so.

Case Study 8.1

CDS

A company, CDS, makes commercial kitchens. The kitchens that CDS makes are energy-efficient and automated. This automation involves robotics, and the introduction of robotics in the commercial kitchens is going to be a new industry wave that we can see moving forward in the next 5 years. The business' value proposition is to "let the chef create." Rather than approaching the market opportunity from one of displacing jobs, it focuses on allowing the chef more time to do what chefs love to do. Energy efficiency is typically controlled or mentioned but there's no real product on the market that allows a business to reduce its overheads and running costs by the introduction of proper thoroughbred energy efficiency that allows them to save more money than it costs to implement. CDS plans to change that.

2. Agile Innovation

One innovation does not make the news forever. Many businesses think they are innovative, but they need deliberate cycles of agile innovation. This becomes essential if they wish keep powering the road from advocacy to authority, and even bad ideas that they don't introduce make the cut.

For example, Elon Musk, CEO of Tesla Motors, and SpaceX, and one of the founders of Paypal, released a press statement in 2013 talking about Hyperloop—a conceptual super-fast train. His SpaceX business is involved in space exploration, and of course coming from Elon Musk, everybody got incredibly excited about the press release. Musk had no intention of developing this technology, but the story travelled around the world and it helped increase his own personal brand warmth.

The second thing we need to be careful of in understanding the term "agile innovation" is that we must have this continued focus. Steve Jobs said:

> People think focus means saying yes to the thing you've got to focus on. But that's not what it means at all. It means saying no to the hundred other good ideas that there are. You have to pick

carefully. I'm actually as proud of the things we haven't done as the things I have done. Innovation is saying no to 1,000 things.

The important thing is keeping the focus on the agile innovation and using agile innovation cycles to usually help deliver solutions to the near-term challenges that have been diagnosed in earlier chapters of this book, the near-term challenges that have been diagnosed in the creation of the strategy.

3. Unique Value Proposition

To become an authority, a business must have a unique value proposition. To stay in advocacy or to move to attention only requires a clear value proposition. To traverse that important X-axis and become an authority requires a unique value proposition as discussed earlier in this book

4. Clear Vision of a Changed Future Well Told

The move from advocacy to authority usually requires the ability to tell stories of how a business' product or service will impact on people's lives. It's not just about the technology, but about telling the story through that technology, of how our product or service will change the future.

This is as important for internal communications as it is for marketing and communicating to the outside world. If everybody in the company is not aligned with the vision and the vision isn't clearly told internally, business people become confused about their goals—this typically leads to fragmentation of the message.

5. Delivery of the Vision

As we're being prophetic and talking about the future, it falls to us to make sure that the future happens. A new formula of paint or new type of propulsion engine doesn't automatically mean that a business becomes the authority—the business must follow through and create the paint or the propulsion engine and have it change the future in the ways it has dictated it will.

6. Leadership: Internally and Externally

Leadership cannot be overstated. As we have mentioned earlier in this book, leadership is so important to formulating and executing good strategy that it is assumed to exist for the purposes of the Seven Principles of Digital Business Strategy.

7. Opinion

In business, we must have opinion. The challenge here is that many businesses don't want to offend one side or the other and it's very difficult to be opinionated without causing offense somewhere. A solicitor's firm, for example, may be backing fathers who are getting divorced but also backing the mothers. They may wish to pioneer one side of the argument but by doing so they alienate the other side. This prevents the business from wanting to have an opinion, but without having an opinion you cannot move. Government organizations are quite often prevented from having an opinion because of their social responsibility and therefore cannot become an authority through innovation.

8. Create Niches and Displace Competitors

Either we have to create a new market niche or we have to displace a competitor if we are to become an authority. The challenge in creating new niches in the market is often that when we look at "Know Your Customer" there is nobody there. The displacement of a competitor means that the competitor needs to be unable to react quickly enough to your innovation. Quite often they're already receiving a disproportionate amount of attention, and we need to decide whether there's room at the authority table for a few competitors.

If you're forging a new marketplace opportunity or creating disruption, there is less inertia in the marketplace, and it's even less if you find that there are waves, emerging technologies or emerging trends. Quite often new niches emerge on a daily basis; they are simply waiting for leadership. Leadership skills combined with an understanding of a new wave could be said to be our essential ingredients.

9. Content that Spreads

Content on our own blog does not make us an authority—being referenced does. We need other independent sources to verify our claims and share our messages. This needs to be echoed in social media, referenced in peer-reviewed publications, and quoted by other authorities in adjacent fields. Tweeters need to tweet and bloggers need to blog about our ideas and reference us. We need to create our own ecosystem and build our own community. We need to be sought after as the keynote speakers at conferences. We need to have offers of partnership because we are now becoming the authority.

10. Involve the Community

We must involve the community and give credit to those that link back to our innovation. We then become the leaders of a community, and we know that we have reached the authority position when other leaders start to emerge within the community itself and go forward.

Case Study 8.2

Aepona were a business that was in a market where they created technology for mobile phone telecommunications operators. They had stayed in advocacy for around 10 years, turning up at trade shows and shaking hands with mobile network operators. The challenge they had was that other companies were in the same market, and they all had product lists of around 130 features, and each of those features lists, while some had better and some worse, were similar. The problem was there were prime and authority brands in Aepona's space. Aepona did the counterintuitive thing of focusing on one specific feature. They spotted a wave happening in the mobile phone market in 2010, whereby mobile phone networks were losing money because people were moving to use voice over Internet protocol programs for their telephone calls, and their voice minutes were reducing.

Part of their technology allowed software developers to create their own apps inside the mobile phone network and to do so safely. This meant that if people wanted to charge their customers using mobile phones, Aepona had the technology to allow software developers to create apps that would enable this—as well as still having 129 other features. They saw the wave coming and decided to become the authority in mobile phone payments from a network perspective. They pioneered the little bit of extra technology that enabled their innovation, narrowed their niche, and moved to authority by speaking to both industry professionals and analysts. They banged the drum around one story about how they were going to be the best, most innovative firm in their community that handled mobile cloud payments from a network operator's perspective, and made sure that their story was being told.

When they became the authority, their earnings went up substantially. This is the feature that many businesses wanted; the mobile networks felt this was the right solution to their dwindling phone minutes problem. An industry competitor came from the prime position and procured the company for $110 million. This valuation had been achieved within 2 years of them dropping the 129 hierarchy features and focusing on one feature.

Now that is, of course, the success story. There are many other waves they could have chosen and they would have missed, so chasing waves is not without risk. It is not without the counterintuitive removal of all our defense mechanisms that we can narrow the niche. When we try to move to authority in a specific niche, quite often the internal politics for a company can be as difficult as the external marketing. People who have been working on features departments for years may no longer see their message being represented by the company as the defining spearhead of moving their authority north. They perceive their own feature as being under threat because it wasn't the innovation driving the company on the road to authority. Handling that political impact is usually helped if we have a clear vision and it is explained to the individuals, and their hierarchy of needs is met before the journey upward begins.

Aepona had set out its vision—it went into great detail explaining where it was going from 2011 to 2012 and how it was going to get there. They had calculated the time, talent, and cash requirements for their baseline before they made any plays, and they ensured they had the resources available to make those plays happen. This was done by creating a very simple table where all the channels they were going to need were listed, and alongside them, the time, talent, and cash they were going to need internally and externally were detailed.

Often what we find is that when businesses create such a table, they realize they don't have the resources and must either narrow their vision further, remain in advocacy, or move to attention. Resources, then, regardless of the size of the business or how well funded the business is, always have a major impact on the play that any business has available to it.

Lastly, and as we mentioned earlier, the website had to change. Aepona changed their website to one that was split into two sections. It was dedicated to handling the customer in one section and their analysts in the other section. They published frequently and used partnerships with other thought leaders in the mobile phone space to help them achieve their outcomes and goals.

CHAPTER 9

The Seventh Principle of Digital Business Strategy— Tactics

The first six of our seven principles involve analysis, investigation, or projection. The seventh is where we decide which tactics we will employ to reach our stated goals and with all the results of our analyses in mind. A tactical plan of action must be tailored very specifically to the results of the first six principles. To show how we create a tactical plan of action, we will examine the Leckey-Firefly Friends case study to illustrate how the information gathered in the first six principles and strategy created from this has translated into tactics.

Case Study 9.1

Established in 1983, Leckey is a globally recognized pioneer in the research, design, and development of clinically focused, posture-supportive products for developmentally challenged children. The company is owned by James Leckey.

Children who benefit from Leckey's products have disabilities such as cerebral palsy, often suffering quite severe movement restrictions, and require specialist equipment to help them to sit up and move. These children require postural assistance, and James' company manufactures wheel chairs that fill that need. Leckey supplies their chairs into the wholesale market via an exclusive contract they have with Ottobock, who supply worldwide. The only exception to this is the National Health Service in the UK, who purchase direct from Leckey.

We met James at a conference where I was doing the keynote speech on digital strategy and he approached me about the possibility of Leckey becoming a "digitally innovative business." He was interested in the difference between doing digital and becoming a digital business as he saw the potential for growth in having a business where the digital elements were written into the business and strategies, merely than adding digital tactics onto their existing business. He also realized that his own business tended toward the latter—it was a business that performed digital tactics, with management giving pointers and encouragement to their digital teams and responding to changes as they arose within the marketplace. His company was striving for likes on Facebook and followers on Twitter, but wasn't using any data or information to make strategic decisions.

Inspired by the realization that he was still performing digital business the old way, James decided that he wished to change to become a digital business. He decided to transform his business, change the practices and culture within his organization, and enable his business to become fast-paced and able to pivot and innovate.

James wanted to begin to cocreate with customers rather than just being customer centric. He wanted to give the management-specific direction and leadership, but understood that he didn't have the knowledge required, himself, to get into the finer detail. He wanted to seek to create market disruptions. He could sense the market was stagnated and was ripe for change, and rather than face disruption he wanted to create market disruption.

He wanted to look at what the near-term business growth challenges were and help his team overcome them. He was interested in understanding the building blocks that allowed businesses to transform.

James understood that strategy was the starting point that would lead to addressing cultural issues and encouraging engagement within the organization, so that people could understand what the business was trying to achieve. He understood that this would lead to realignment of many of the departments and that there were senior executives that would need further education if they were to lead teams and break down challenges into more detailed projects and tasks. If the business wanted continued growth, James understood that agile innovation would have to become an essential part of the business and that agile innovation would require the business to collaborate with customers and third parties. This had never happened in his business. Innovation had always occurred internally, without the assistance of partners or customers. He understood that all things in turn would have to result in his senior leadership giving great direction to their teams, so that those teams could perform to the top of their ability.

Technology was simply accepted as being a part of the process. James accepted that it would be omnipresent throughout each of the stages of formulating his strategy and transforming his business. Using the Seven Principles of Digital Business Strategy, James and his team got their transformation rolling.

The first principle they tackled was "Know Yourself." The diagnosis came quite easily—James realized that the distribution channel had his sales maximized; he was at the mercy of Ottobock and its distribution arm. The supply chain between him and the customer was beyond his control. Ottobock sold to primary care trusts who then recommended the products to therapists who in turn prescribed the products to the parents of children who needed them.

James' business was coasting, and he had a desire for change. Despite having lots of ideas for innovation that he wished to test, the current distribution method he was using, and the market to which he was selling via that distribution method remained constrained. He liked the idea of running a digital, more modern business and had seen many of his other businesses succeed and enjoy growth, either through beginning as digitally innovative businesses or through transforming into digitally innovative businesses through effective strategy.

Eventually, through a lot of consultation and soul searching, the ambition became "to create a new market for direct-to-parent family products for children with disabilities." To create a new market means there is no current market in existence. As discussed earlier in this book, this cuts out many of the moves within the quadrant. We cannot, for example, go straight to advertising or seek pay-per-click attention, because nobody is searching for a product that they don't yet know exists.

James and his team worked hard on developing a value proposition. They looked at their internal and external value proposition before creating marketing messages and sought out their differentiator to make their value proposition unique. The first proposition they came up with was "we are the pioneers in early participation therapy for children with special needs, because we produce affordable, clinically excellent products, better than anyone else." They arrived at this value proposition because they had always dealt directly with the medical profession. They always had to produce clinically excellent products, but upon contemplation they realized the new customer, when they were selling to parents directly, was not a medical professional. They needed another, more fitting differentiator.

Eventually, James and his team decided upon the value proposition "we are the pioneers in early participation therapy for children with special needs because we make stuff that involves the family in helping the child engage in life better than anyone else." This softer language and focus toward the child was the guiding internal messaging that would help marketers and help other departments to understand exactly what its purpose was when the business was to move forward.

James had chosen the term "early participation therapy" in the hope this could be the new wave that his business could help create. It didn't turn out that way. When he checked the market and entered the term into a search engine, he found that there were already many scholarly articles that used this term, which were already created and cited. This meant that James' business could not create the phrase and dominate it in search engines, which meant that they couldn't protect it. There were already heavily cited, referenced articles on the web that would likely trump James' business if they went with this term for their wave creation and found themselves in a more prime status within the marketplace. "Family involved participation" was the term that James' business eventually decided would feed their internal value proposition, after some market research.

Next, James looked at the customer. He decided that because he was creating a new marketplace, and therefore lacked existing customers to consult, he would collaborate with third parties to better understand what the concerns and needs of the parents and carers of children with mobility needs were in day-to-day life. Cerebra is a charity that helps improve the lives of children with brain-related conditions, and they helped explain all of the challenges that parents and carers face when they take children on everyday outings, like shopping, eating out, and playing on a park swing.

James and his team set about working with Cerebra to come up with their first product. Since they were going to sell directly to parents, they could bypass therapists and the channel and didn't need to be prescribed.

The first product the company came up with was the Goto seat, and they offered a 7 percent commission to Cerebra as an acknowledgment for their contribution in creating the product. The business set about the design and manufacture of this first seat, while the marketers set about creating right environment to sell product directly to parents.

When they looked at the competitors in the marketplace, the business realized there were no direct competitors, but there were many indirect competitors—other sites were selling products to parents for their child with special needs. Some had quite a large *force*, but few had the idea of production facilities. They were online retailers but weren't able to adapt and create products should a new market entrant come in to play. Other competitors were too big to be bothered by a new entrant in a new marketplace. Each of the companies was identified as a threat and alerts were set up to monitor their activity, because James' business understood that if they created market penetration, these other businesses would try to copy or move into the market. Defense mechanisms needed to be set up if the business was to achieve market dominance and become an authority or prime player.

James and his team looked at the engine of growth. While it would have been easy for them to go with partners in the attention category, they realized they had something more unique, which could gain them attention in their own right, perhaps even allowing them to traverse the X-axis and become an authority.

James went through his checklist of the 10 characteristics required for a business to become an authority and realized that his business had what it took. He decided not to go down the attention route, even though it would have brought a lot of easy wins early on. Instead, he decided to aim to become an authority. Once that engine of growth had been selected, it was time to set up all of the base camp tools—the processes, training, and tactics—that would be needed to enable the business to become an authority in the identified, emerging wave.

The business set about understanding staff training and culture. They also had to address a channel conflict, since they had an existing contract of exclusivity with Ottobock. They made technology choices, performed blogger outreach, and tested for demand. They sought peer review engagement, performed propensity to purchase modeling within customer sections, testing what the likely conversion of interest-to-purchase might be.

If the Goto seat was to become a seller and make good profit, the business would need to perform therapist inductions and gain the backing of therapists. They needed to understand what sizes of the Goto seat they were going to sell, and this information all had to come from analysis. In the early days of base camp, the business set out their "leap of faith" assumptions and identified the mile markers that would be required to get the business into a position to become an authority. Each of those mile markers was set and broken down into tasks.

The business knew it would eventually need to engage further with bloggers, find international speaking engagements to participate in, and so on, but it knew that all of these things were future potentials that would really depend on what happened more immediately. For this reason, the business did not dwell on the larger, future opportunities, but looked instead to its more near-term challenges. The challenges that needed to be solved immediately before the business could move forward.

To create its tactical plan, the business created a table that showed all the mile markers. Each of the mile markers broke down into projects and the projects into tasks. Each of the mile markers had an owner, so that the owner can oversee its completion, and each project was allocated to a senior manager.

One mile marker may require more than one project to be met. The projects may be overseen by different managers, but there is always an owner for each mile marker, and there is always an owner for each project. Once projects are defined, their overseers can then break them down into smaller tasks and allocate them to their teams. The teams are shown the vision and given understanding of the wider strategy. Major mile markers are shared with the teams in order that they can see the full vision for the company and understand what the business is trying to do and the part they play in it.

If the tasks are deemed to be true digital tasks, then empirical analyses are performed so the business can gather data to help them understand if the task has been accomplished to within the project's required parameters.

The business set about getting some baseline facts and figures in play so the business could understand the starting point, with as little assumption as possible, before it moved forward. The more assumption can be taken out of the strategy (and thus projects and tasks) the better. Multiplying assumptions causes greater errors and creates more risk.

When James knew the near-term mile markers, projects, and tasks, he went to his board to seek the resources that were required. The resources required ended up being greater than either he or the board had initially anticipated and much greater than the board was prepared to sink into a test project.

James broke down tactical resources into time, talent, and cash. He broke down the channels and how many man days it would take to help him achieve the tactical outcomes that were required for many of the projects and tasks. The board eventually gave James the resources he needed, and he set about tackling his first mile marker—the channel conflict arising from the exclusivity deal with Ottobock. Rather than tackling the legal issues of that contract, James decided to set up a separate business entity to test out the Goto seat. The company was named Firefly Friends, and the business set out to market the Goto seat in conjunction with Cerebra. Very early on, people started sharing pictures of the Goto seat on social media. These pictures depicted children who would normally have had to sit with carers, due to their mobility needs, participating in family life better than they had before.

The story started to spread and customers started to search for the Goto seat by name. Very quickly, the business had built up a healthy number of visitors—around 18,000 per month—and they were all coming from social channels, direct channels, referral channels, and organic search. It was notable that the social media driving their traffic was the social media of other people, and not of Firefly itself. Their content had been syndicated, and it was the act of syndication that led to new customers. James understood that for the strategy to continue to develop, he needed to get business alignment and the culture of the business exactly right.

Having taken Firefly as a different entity, he then created new departments. These departments differed from those of his traditional business, and the differences reflected the digital nature of Firefly. The departments he chose were Community and Education, Innovation, Production, Marketing, Customer Service, and Administration.

James met his requirement for agile innovation by recruiting those around him that he felt were thought leaders in the area. His next collaboration was with a lady called Debbie Elnatan—an Israeli woman who had come up with an ingenious invention that firefly called the Upsee. The Upsee is a mobility harness device that lets children with motor impairment stand and walk with the help of an adult. James engaged with the community around him by inviting all the top journalists and bloggers in the field to come to his factory to get a prerelease launch view of the Upsee and to allow them to test it.

Shortly before the release of the Upsee they started to talk passionately about this new product and how it could change the child's environment. They talked about how the Upsee could enable "family involved participation" (our wave term) in a way that no product before it had.

The number of visits to the website instantly rose dramatically from 18,000 to 200,000. Of these, 87,000 were from social media, 48,000 from direct hits, and 33,000 from referral traffic; 27,000 came from organic search and 2,500 from other means. The Upsee was picked up by mainstream media, who shared the story of the Upsee. Children with limited mobility were now able to perform and help with everyday tasks and activities, like stacking a dishwasher, kicking a ball, or going for a walk. The story of the Upsee was syndicated on many news channels. It appeared in over 100 countries on television and on hundreds of websites, in hundreds of languages around the world. The Upsee went viral.

Nobody could predict that the Upsee would go any more viral than the earlier product, the Goto seat. It happened through experimentation and innovation, but the more innovative a business is, the more innovative products or services it has, the better it solves a customer task—the more the business' traffic builds.

Firefly's Upsee now easily gains 150,000 unique visitors every month and has a very healthy conversion rate. It has built a brand of its own and is a prime player in the field of family participation products for children with special needs, and no competitor has been able to disrupt it. Undoubtedly, the unique product plays a large part in Firefly's success, but the products came from of collaborative design because of James' desire to create a solution that fitted in with Firefly being a digital business. If James hadn't set out to create a digital business—if he had gone the traditional route and sold through a distributor and used his own social media channels as superfluous add-ons, the Upsee would not have gone viral.

James set out to reimagine how his business could be and to develop a business that was going to be successful by disrupting a marketplace. Therapists have come on board with Firefly and are now starting to understand more about how the products are helping children in cognitive and physical development. Other products have now started to emerge, all created and conceived by the community, and designed and built by Firefly, who in turn gives credit back to the community.

The formula James would say he has gone through to create a successful business was that he started with a digital business strategy that allowed him to share his vision. He was able to break that down and understand the customers and the marketplace. He was able to align the business and get the culture right internally, able to educate his board, and able to look for agile innovation. All of these things, combined with his vision, lead to mile markers, projects, and tasks, which in turn, when executed by a properly informed, well-educated people base, led to tactical excellence. James didn't start with tactics first—he started with strategy first. The business is now growing rapidly and may someday overtake his legacy Leckey business in terms of size.

James used the Seven Principles of Digital Business Strategy to identify a new market niche, create a digital business with a new structure and digital processes, create an industry wave, create agile innovation cycles, reach new customers, and make a market move north to authority.

CHAPTER 10

Conclusion

This book has drawn from over 120 business case studies through Ireland, UK, and Europe as well as academic research over the past two decades conducted in the UK, the United States, and Australia. The goal has been to provide an answer as to how to create digital business strategy.

As you are now aware this is essentially business strategy created and implemented through the lens of digital. Interestingly in a few years the title of this book will be redundant—it will be rechristened the Seven Principles of Business Strategy with the "digital" word no longer emphasized. In many ways, this future change reinforces where many businesses today are going wrong—they are obsessing about the technology and being defined by it rather focusing on leveraging value from the technology in delivering differential and innovative value propositions to customers. Our society has become a technopoly—we are taking our orders from technology and our authorization from technology (see work of Neil Postman for more on this concept). The issue, hopefully evident to you now having read this book, is that the opportunity does not lie within the technology per se but rather in the way that technology is leveraged to cocreate value with customers. That requires a marketing-oriented and strategic approach.

By looking through the lens of digital, we propose digital modeling frameworks, we explore and understand business alignment challenges cultural challenges, and we explore competency gaps that may act as barriers to success in this new context.

We must understand the ground rules and be able to make a distinction between businesses that do digital and digital businesses. The digital businesses are the ones that are winning. Senior managers can run digital businesses without fully understanding the inner workings of the technology to do so. The Seven Principles of Digital Business Strategy provides a framework where all strategic options are explored and directions proposed and explained. Whatever your business context and whatever your level of digital competency, this book will hopefully add value to your business in our digitized economy.

Index

OTHER TITLES IN DIGITAL AND SOCIAL MEDIA MARKETING AND ADVERTISING COLLECTION

Victoria L. Crittenden, Babson College, *Editor*

- *Corporate Branding in Facebook Fan Pages: Ideas for Improving Your Brand Value* by Eliane Pereira Zamith Brito, Maria Carolina Zanette, Benjamin Rosenthal, Carla Caires Abdalla, and Mateus Ferreira
- *Presentation Skills: Educate, Inspire and Engage Your Audience* by Michael Weiss
- *The Connected Consumer* by Dinesh Kumar
- *Mobile Commerce: How It Contrasts, Challenges and Enhances Electronic Commerce* by Esther Swilley
- *Email Marketing in a Digital World: The Basics and Beyond* by Richard C. Hanna, Scott D. Swain and Jason Smith
- *R U #SoLoMo Ready?: Consumers and Brands in the Digital Era* by Stavros Papakonstantinidis, Athanasios Poulis and Prokopis Theodoridis
- *Social Media Marketing: Strategies in Utilizing Consumer-Generated Content* by Emi E. Moriuchi
- *Fostering Brand Community Through Social Media* by William F. Humphrey, Jr., Debra A. Laverie and Shannon B. Rinaldo
- *#Share: How to Mobilize Social Word of Mouth (sWOM)* by Natalie T. Wood and Caroline K. Muñoz

Announcing the Business Expert Press Digital Library

Concise e-books business students need for classroom and research

This book can also be purchased in an e-book collection by your library as

- *a one-time purchase,*
- *that is owned forever,*
- *allows for simultaneous readers,*
- *has no restrictions on printing, and*
- *can be downloaded as PDFs from within the library community.*

Our digital library collections are a great solution to beat the rising cost of textbooks. E-books can be loaded into their course management systems or onto students' e-book readers. The **Business Expert Press** digital libraries are very affordable, with no obligation to buy in future years. For more information, please visit **www.businessexpertpress.com/librarians.** To set up a trial in the United States, please email **sales@businessexpertpress.com.**